# A Research from the Business Operation's Perspective

I'd like to thank Mag. Friedrich Urbanek for his generous sharing of his knowledge and long-term experience in the financial risk management, and I'd also like to thank Dr.Martin Bartels, the partner of LightFin, Drs. Patrick Mijnals, the founder of Bettervest, for helping me with getting an industrial insider view. Ultimately I'd like to thank my family for supporting me constantly. Thank you.

Xiaoshuai Yuan

# The Risk Management in Crowdfunding

## How could intermediaries reduce risks for Crowdfunding participants?

1 Auflage

Autor: Xiaoshuai, Yuan
Umschlaggestaltung, Illustration: Xiaoshuai, Yuan
Lektorat, Korrektorat: Friedrich, Urbanek

Verlag: tredition GmbH, Hamburg
ISBN: 978-3-7323-7810-4 (Paperback)
ISBN: 978-3-7323-7811-1 (Hardcover)
Printed in Germany

# Index

# Preface

This book is designed to give an introduction of the new funding model „crowdfunding", which developed rapidly since the Internet becomes ubiquitous and diversified. Crowdfunding describes the fund-raising for a project or an idea through numerous individuals via online platform. In recent years, crowdfunding excite interest intrigue all over the world, becomes an issue of concern in the regulation. The number of platforms is multiplied up every year, provided services become diversified and mature.

During the financial crisis, traditional financing channels tighten up on their investments, crowdfunding becomes an alternative scheme. This research is made during the recovery of global financial crises, in this time period the banking industry bears financial distress, and is requested more liquidity by Basel III regulation or small business administration in the US. The funding for innovative business projects, for small and medium sized enterprises (SMEs) become more difficult. Although a lot of researches confirm that economic contributions and job creation are mainly made by SMEs. To solve the financing difficulty, crowdfunding becomes a feasible solution.

Ordinarily crowdfunding is used in the initial funding or early-stage financing, both involve in high risks. Crowdfunding industry is still in its early stage of development, appropriate shareholders and stakeholders' protection mechanism not only benefits entrepreneurs, investors and platforms, but also has great significance for the industry itself. Platforms adopt various methods to reduce risks, although approaches are based on the general risk management theory and the risk management technique. This research devotes its focus on analyses of crowdfunding specific risks from different perspectives, possibilities that crowdfunding platforms as the intermediary minimize risks for both entrepreneurs and investors, and how could they do that.

Crowdfunding industry is still in its infancy[1], very little data and researches exist concerning this new form of funding which might be found in the academic sphere. The existing disquisitions and researches mostly have macro-

[1] European Crowdfundfunding Network 2013: 9

economic perspective, which provide the bibliographic basic for the theoretical analyses. The current state of researches increases the difficulty of qualitative investigation for this research. However, some platforms offer information about their ways of investors' protection, which is used as information source to answer the research question. Simultaneously there is a multitude of online news, discussions, blogs in Internet, which offers information and data, and will be taken into consideration very cautiously, because their information has expected aberrance, its accuracy and reliability are hard to verify. I have also interviewed crowdfunding two operators to win an insider aspect, to collect and summarize ideas.

The research is structured into 2 main parts. In the first chapter, we give a concise overview about the Internet-based financial industry, its basic theories and introduce some models. The second chapter focuses on the Crowdfunding and gives an overview of the current regulatory state from differently developing markets: US, Europe and China, to introduce business environment from macro-economic perspective. Ultimately this Chapter summarizes characteristics and actual challenges based on the previous detection. The following chapter leads into risk management theory, introduce the concept of risk management in finance and the conventional risk management process. The second part offers important insights about crowdfunding specific risks, and answer the research question „Could crowdfunding platforms reduce risks for the participants? And how could they reach this goal? "with selected cases. The last part of this research sums up the findings and proposes possibilities to support the future development of crowdfunding industry.

# Chapter 1 - Introduction of Internet based Finance

In the information era, resources become the key factor for success, consumers are not only the target, but also the co-creator of value[2]. Powered social and organizational networks turn to a strong social network. Also in the financial services, consumer's role has expanded.

The foundation of the Internet-based finance is the rapid popularization of Internet; the diffusion rate has outstripped the branch network of traditional financial institutions in the past decade. With the increase of applied value in the daily life, Internet diversified its field of application and emerged prodigious potential. The combination of Internet platform, mobile devices, data technology and financial service comes out with the synergy, and satisfies different market.

From the technological point of view, the new generation of web search engines, big data, crowd computing, social networking etc. realizes the fundamental change in the applied environment, „combine human intelligence (the crowd) with artificial intelligence (the cloud) in order to produce quality results at unprecedented speed"[3]. More connections, raising meaning of collaborative individuals precipitate the „crowdsourcing"[4], which is taken advantages from Internet-based finance to increase the availability, the instantaneity and the convenience of financial services.

From the economic perspective, the financing is critical for the real economy, but in the current state, the capital allocation is imbalance, individuals and SMEs have enormous financing demand. On the other hand, a huge amount of private equity seeks for efficient investment channels. The financial services have diversified with a numerous of innovations in payment, financing, asset

---

2 cf. Kambil et al. 1999: 43

3 Wifipedia <http://en.wikipedia.org/wiki/Crowd_computing>, date of access: 08.08.2014

4 Wifipedia < http://en.wikipedia.org/wiki/Crowdsourcing>, date of access: 08.08.2014

management, investment etc., and are qualitatively changed thru the Internet's convergence effect.

Source: Business circle: Economics Transformation Program[5]

Internet-based finance has some features:

- Information processing is based on online information collection and data technologies:

All messages included the information which has no obligation to be revealed are gathered from Internet, especially online social networks. The information is restructured, analyzed, and applied for valuation. In the Internet-based finance, all information about initiators and investors is collected from the social media, reorganized and standardized by the web search engine, and becomes a continuous, mutative index. This database is than adopted to measure the

[5]Business circle < http://www.businesscircle.com.my/smes-cloud-union-made/>. date of access: 02.12.2015

probability of default, for the risk-based pricing etc.

The Internet based information processing basically satisfies information demands, reduces the information asymmetry and information costs, and is capable to substitute main functions of commercial banks, rating agencies.

- Supply and demand meet directly via Internet:

Internet-based finance inherits the characteristics of Internet, which is decentralized, democratic, selectable, it allows funders to select initiator or project, to decide for investment models and amount etc. by own choices without intermediaries' influence.

Internet plays the abstract intermediary role, could efficiently avoid the intermediary related risks e.g. bank bankruptcy, reduce the intermediary costs, enhances the spontaneous profitability of financial activities. It triggers the change in the resource allocation and the pricing structure of financial services.

Exhibit 1. Financing Process within and without traditional intermediary

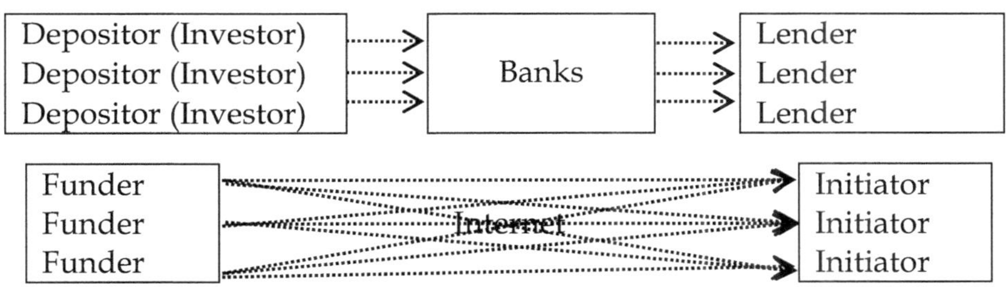


- Internet-based finance puts great emphasis on collaborated power (the crowd):

As distinct from the traditional allocation of sources, the central thought of Internet-based finance is to give full power to the collaboration. Centralized capital flow disperses risks by bigger undertakers' base, reduces risks of individual investors, realizes the financing for innovative projects and venturesome start-ups, optimizes the entrepreneurial environment and the living condition of creative industries.

- The simplification of products attracts more participators:

As mentioned in the last paragraph, Internet-based finance reduces individual risks by collaborating investments, therefore demands for risk hedging decrease. Investors do not have to use complicated securities to hedge risks. In the chapter 4, Internet elicited specific risks and risk management approaches are introduced in details.

- Well-established infrastructure and online operating reduce the transaction cost:

Transaction costs can be identified into 3 categories: search and information costs, bargaining and decision costs, policing and enforcement costs[67]. Transparent information, access to sources of projects and enterprises, standardized and simplified tradeoff process, minimized agency costs and management fee allow investors benefit much more from their invested capital.

The concept of Internet-based finance has simultaneously emerged within the development of PC and Internet in the 80s with the „home banking "idea from banks and other traditional financial institutions. In 1983, the Nottingham Building Society launched the first Internet banking service in UK, which shaped the basis for the Internet banking construction. In 1994, the US based financial institution Stanford Federal Credit Union developed its online banking service. The online banking has entered into the period of rapid expansion due to the technology development, online banking become prevalent.

Since millennium, since traditional financial institutions extend their services via web, Internet companies enter the market, seize the initiative, and take market share with their technical advantages and customer base. They utilize e-commerce platforms, mobile payment, big data, crowd computing, social media etc. to infiltrate their services into finance, and to broaden the range of

---

[6] Dahlman (1979): 22

[7] Wikipedi <http://en.wikipedia.org/wiki/Transaction_cost>, date of access: 08.08.2014

business.

In recent years, Internet-based finance is identified as an independent industry, is positioned for the strategic competition from both traditional financial institutions and Internet companies. Not only in US and UK, but also in China, the most dominant privately owned e-commerce business giant Alibaba Group provides financial services through Yu'e Bao via peer-to-peer Lending and crowdfunding[8], and gain ¥1230 billion in ten months.

Internet-based finance is still in its rapid growth and changes the competitive state. Diversified models e.g. third-party payment, P2P, crowdfunding emerge endlessly, and change consumer' habits. Based on the sources allocation, costs can be reduced efficiently, and covers the shortage of traditional financial services in a certain extent.

---

[8] cf. Alipay: < https://financeprod.alipay.com/fund/index.htm>, date of access: 30.07.2014

## Chapter 1.1 - The Theory of Internet-based Finance

Allocation of capital is the main function of financial services. In the traditional finance, intermediaries have advantages of economies of scales, professional skills and information resources, which help them relieve the information asymmetry between depositor and money raisers. Financial intermediaries play important roles in the allocation of resources and make valuable contributions for the real economy. But they also demand enormous transaction costs, which include profits, taxes incoming, salary, and so on.

Internet- based finance processes the information through the modern information technology. Information sources are generated and disseminated in online social networks, reorganized and sorted by search engines. The cloud computing ensures the high-speed processing and the continuous dynamic data providing with low costs. These sequences of data can be used for the assessment of default probability and risk- based pricing, satisfy the information demand of financial activities. The Internet- based information technology has the capability to replace the main function of traditional intermediaries. A good example from the US peer-to-peer lending company Lending Club, which had funded $6.2 billion in loans and paid over $595 million interest to investors[9]. Lending Club implements the internal credit grade evaluation for each case, based on the borrower's credit scores, loan amount, last six-months' history, debt to income ratio. Lending Club assigns a credit grade to each approved loan, which determines the interest rate. The credit grade corresponds to different interest rate, lower the credit rating, higher the interest payment.

The foundation of Internet-based finance is online payment. Along with the popularization of mobile devises and the development of mobile communication technologies, the mobile payment integrates with online banking and other electronic payment methods, the convergence of Internet and mobile

---

[9] Lending Club homepage <https://www.lendingclub.com/public/about-us.action>, date of access: 11.01.2015

communication becomes the trend.

Driven by the popularization of mobile payment, the maturation of online information processing and the rapid development of modern information technology, direct financial activities between individuals break the traditional industrial boundaries. On conditions, that the information is almost symmetric for both funders and borrowers, transaction costs are relative low, the platform plays a role as the intermediary to satisfy a wide range of demands from both funders and lenders' sides, and enable „a possibility of completion of total transactions between one or more Initiators and funders, where the maximum acceptable interest payment of Initiators is higher than the minimum acceptable payoff of funders“ [10]. This theory is verified with a simplified formulation:

- The calculation of maximum acceptable interest payment of initiators

We assume, that a lender „i“ belongs to a initiators' group $i \in I$, who has equity „$E_i$“, demands a loan „$L_i$“ with the interest rate „$r_i$“ to start a project with the expected return „$Exp.R_i$“, the probability of making profit is represented with „$P_i$“, the probability of 0 profit is „$(1- P_i)$“. The debt/equity ratio is represented with „$l_i$ “. The expected Profit is calculated with:

$$\frac{(1+Exp.Ri)(Ei+Li)}{Pi} \text{ or } 0$$

$$Exp.\,Ri = \text{Rate of expected return}$$

$$E_i = \text{Equity}$$

$$L_i = \text{Loan}$$

$$Pi = \text{Probability of making profit}$$

If the lender does not take any loan, his/her assets will remain the same $E_i$. It makes sense to take a loan, only if the expected return is higher than Ei, after paying loan and interest:

$$\frac{(1+Exp.Ri)(Ei+Li)}{Pi} - (1+r_i)\, L_i \geq E_i$$

$$r_i = \text{Interest rate}$$

If the project fails, the expected return can be calculated with (1+ Exp. Ri)(Ei +

[10] Xie et al. 2012: 27

Li) − Pi(1+ $r_i$ ) $L_i$, which leads to the condition of taking loan:

$$(1+ \text{Exp. Ri})(\text{Ei} + \text{Li}) - \text{Pi}(1+ r_i)\, L_{i,} \geq E_i$$

Where the maximum acceptable interest rate $r_i$ is:

$$\frac{1+\text{Exp.Ri}+\text{Exp.Ri}/\text{li}}{\text{Pi}} - 1 \geq r_i$$

$$l_i = \text{debt/equity ratio}$$

- The calculation of minimum acceptable payoff of funders:

We assume, that the funder „f" represents the funders' group f∈F, who has the opportunity cost „$r_f$", he/she is interested in lending the loan to „i". This deal produces transaction costs, which is paid for the clearing and the credit evaluation. Transaction costs are normally correlated with the loan amount, the relationship is represented with„$C_{ij}= \frac{Transaction\ cost}{Li}$", „$C_{ij}$" >0.

Although the credit evaluation is made, the funder still has to take the account of the information asymmetry, which affects the probability of payoff. The deviation is represented with „$\lambda_{ij}$". The probability of being payoffed from funder's perspective is calculated with:

$$\lambda_{ij})\ \text{Pi},\ \lambda_{ij} \in (0,1)$$

The condition of lending is that, the interest payment is higher than the opportunity return „$r_f$". Considering the default possibility, the funder will get payoff by (1-$\lambda_{ij}$) Pi, the expected payoff is calculated with:

$$(1- \lambda_{ij})\ \text{Pi}\ (1+ r_i)\ L_i$$

Transaction costs have to be taken into consideration, therefore the lending is only executed, if:

$$(1-\lambda_{ij})\ Pi\ (1+r_i)\ L_i - C_{ij}\ L_i \geq (1+r_f)\ L_i$$

By the formula derivation, we get the minimum acceptable payoff of funder:

$$\frac{Cij+1+rf}{(1-\lambda ij)\ Pi} - 1 \geq r_i$$

The condition of the deal's existent is that, the maximum acceptable interest payment of initiators is higher than the minimum acceptable payoff of funders, which is:

$$\frac{1+Exp.Ri+Exp.Ri/li}{Pi} - 1 \geq \frac{Cij+1+rf}{(1-\lambda ij)\ Pi} - 1$$

The formula is transformed as:

$$C_{ij} + (1+ Exp.Ri + Exp.Ri/li)\ \lambda ij \leq Exp.Ri + Exp.Ri/li - rf$$

In this formula, $C_{ij}$ and $\lambda_{ij}$ are related to both lenders and funders. On the condition, that other parameters are constant, the smaller the transaction cost $C_{ij}$, the smaller the information asymmetry $\lambda_{ij}$, the bigger the chance of deal. „The set of possibilities of transactions" is formulated as:

$$\{(i,j) \mid i \in I, f \in F, C_{ij} + (1+ Exp.Ri + Exp.Ri/li)\ \lambda ij \leq Exp.Ri + Exp.Ri/li - rf\}$$

The concept explains, the less the information asymmetry, the more the probabilities of total transaction; the smaller the transaction cost, the bigger the probabilities of total transaction. Compare to traditional financial activities, Internet-based finance has the features such as lower transaction cost and gigantic information sources. We assume that, transaction costs and information asymmetric can be approximately ignored. „The possibility of completion of total transactions " is formulated as:

$$\{(i,j) \mid i \in I, f \in F, Exp.\,Ri + Exp.\,Ri/\,li \geq rf\}$$

Which shows that, the set of possibility of completion of total transactions might exist in Internet-based finance.

## Chapter 1.2 - Introduction of some Models

The Internet-based Finance develops several models, we focus on the Peer-to-Peer Lending, Crowdfunding and the Third-Party Payment.

- Peer-to-Peer Lending (P2P Lending)

The P2P Lending is a lending behavior between individuals, without going through the traditional financial intermediary such as banks[11].

The rapid development of P2P Lending has the background, that traditional financial institutions have not solved financing problems of many individuals, who have imperfect credit rating but prepare to pay more interest.

With the rapid development of Internet technology, online P2P lending platforms emerged, P2P Lending transformed gradually from offline model into O2O model (online to offline). Today's P2P Lending is a direct financing activity through a third-party online platform. The platforms allow borrowers publish lending requests, offer information about borrowers' credit ratings, charge a management fee. This debtor-creditor relationship is formed outside traditional financial institutions, what this model requests, is a developed credit rating system.

From the perspective of the business model, P2P Lending and Crowdfunding are compatible, that both modes are executed through online platforms, and connect Initiator and funders. P2P requests a interest payment for their capital, and crowdfunding investments profit a reward or a financial payoff. From the investors' perspective, both modes constitute the synergy to establish an investment portfolio, thereby the risks are minimized on the condition of risk diversification.

Commonly recognized first P2P Lending platform is Zopa from UK, which was found in 2005[12]. The Ratesetter is another successful platform, which is famous for its Provision Fund and 100% track record of protecting lenders

---

[11] Wikipedia <http://en.wikipedia.org/wiki/Peer-to-peer_lending>, date of access: 18.01.2015

[12] Zopa <http://www.zopa.com/about>, date of access: 18.01.2015

from the default. Lending Works is a player since 2012, who protects their lenders with insurance against the default risk.

source: Bach: Fieldnotes [13]

In the US, the first P2P Lending platform is the San Francisco-based Prosper, which was founded in 2006. Prosper collects capital and distributes them for loans. The investments' opportunities are unsecured, but it provides lenders a mass of information such as borrower risk scores built on historical data. The platform also provides a „Prosper Rating" to offer figures of estimated average of annual default rate. In 2008, the Securities and Exchange Commission (SEC) considers Prosper as a provider of financial securities, platforms are required to file the registration statement with the SEC[14]. Another San Francisco-based P2P Lending platform Lending Club also registered since 2012, Lending Club

[13] Bach < http://jonathanbach.me/fieldnotes/2015/7/22/peer-pressure-peer-to-peer-lending-is-changing-the-game>, date of access: 02.12.2015

[14] cf. Chapmen and Cutler LLP 2014: 7

becomes the largest credit marketplace in US and funded more than 6 billion US dollars in loans and paid nearly 600 million dollars interest (statistics as of 30th.September 2014)[15]. To reduce the default risk, Lending Club only allows borrowers with FICO score of 660 or higher to apply for loans, 90% of applications are declined and higher interest rates are assigned to riskier loans[16].

China is another dynastic market for the online P2P Lending. The reason is that the offline P2P lending is well developed for centuries, in past decades, it became the most popular way to finance SMEs. Since the first online platform has arisen in 2006, the number of platforms grows rapidly. Till June 2014, there were 1200 online P2P Lending platforms in China.

Compare to the traditional lending, online P2P Lending has characteristics, that deals can be operated simply, the information asymmetry is relative small, and transaction costs are low, the interest rate is visually connected with the risk lever.

- Crowdfunding

"Crowdfunding can be defined as a collective effort of many individuals who network and pool their resources to support efforts initiated by other people or organizations. This is usually done via or with the help of the Internet. "[17]

Based on the Web 2.0 technology, „users interact and collaborate with each other in a social media dialogue as creator of user-generated content in a virtual community"[18]. Some as the Wikipedia, which offers an open online community, every individual can post applications and information to a number of other users.

Crowdfunding is initially used to finance creative ideas, a group of funders subscribes to an initiator to support an innovative project. In return, funders get nothing or rewards such as a product of the funded project. In last few years, start-ups and SMEs start to raise fund via crowdfunding, the equity

---

[15] Lendingclub <https://www.lendingclub.com>, date of access: 18.01.2015

[16] Wikipedia <http://en.wikipedia.org/wiki/Lending_Club>, date of access: 18.01.2015

[17] cf. De Buysere et al. 2012: 9

[18] O'Reilly 2005: <Scholar.googleusercontent.com >, date of access: 05.08.2014

based crowdfunding and debt based crowdfunding appear. They attract a lot of attention of regulation in various countries.

Source: The Startup Garage: Pros of Crowdfunding[19]

- The online third-party transaction

"The third-party transaction is a business deal involving a buyer, a seller and a third party. The third party's involvement varies with the type of business

[19] The Startup Garage< https://thestartupgarage.com/pros-crowdfunding/>, date of access: 02.12.2015

transaction[20]." The third party is usually the online payment portal, who is not affiliated with either buyer or seller. It uses the communication technology, computer science and information security technology, establishes an automated connection between users and Bank payment system, based on the agreement with banks. The third- party transaction has a wide range of utilizations, it's not only used for the online payment, but also used for the mobile payment, O2O business models, and is widely used in the e-commerce. PayPal is an often-used third party portal worldwide, Alipay from Alibaba is the most popular online payment portal in China. The third-party online transaction service provider gains from transaction costs, interest from the deposit and customized solution services.

The rise of third party transaction brings challenges to the traditional bank transaction service. The relationship between the online payment portal and commercial banks changes from total cooperation to the composition of competition and cooperation. During the development of technology, third-party portal becomes incredibly powerful. It gradually involves in financial services such as fund business, insurance business, asset management business etc. It benefits from the accumulated personal data and transaction data, in cooperation with other institutes, the payment portal is able to offer loan with better rate or other customized services. It continuously expands its scope of business, overlaps the core business field of traditional financial institutes, forces bank to face the competition.

---

[20] Investopedia< http://www.investopedia.com/terms/t/third-party-transaction.asp>, date of access: 18.01.2015

# Chapter 2 - Crowdfunding

Since 2008, the global financial crises embittered financial institutions with distress. The SMEs had to face tight lending conditions, therefore in the broadest sense, the access to capital became difficult. A new form of financing crowdfunding realizes investors and enterprises to meet via online intermediaries- platforms.

## Chapter 2.1 - The Concept of Crowdfunding

"Crowdfunding is the practice of funding a project or venture by raising monetary contributions from a large number of people, typically via the Internet."[21]

Crowdfunding contributes an alternative approach to raise fund for innovative projects, SMEs, start-ups, which allows initiators introduce, promote their business ideas and absorb capital directly from a large numbers of individuals via the intermediary e.g. crowdfunding platforms. Funders can finance collaboratively, they provide money with different motivations, e.g. financial return, shareholding in projects, material rewards etc. Crowdfunding platforms play a very important role, and bring entrepreneurs and funders together.

Crowdfunding has various application fields, is used for financing all commercial or private needs, including fields, where initiators are not able to raise money for. Election, implementation of creative ideas, financing startups, personal finance needs, donation and charities, rebuilding the factories, environmental protection, pre-selling real estates, technological development and researches etc. have been already funded via crowdfunding. Most of platforms focus on a narrow business field, where they can centralize and allocate their resource.

Different platforms allow various amounts of funding, donation and rewards based crowdfunding platforms have usually funded projects between several

[21] Direct quote: <http://www.oxforddictionaries.com/us/definition/american_english/crowdfunding>, date of access: 30.07.2014

thousand U.S. dollars and 100 thousand US dollars. Equity based funding projects have higher targets, up to 100 thousand US dollars.

The rapid development of crowdfunding profits much from the Internet technology and the large number of Internet users, which forms the natural user-base for crowdfunding. Financial needs are the other factors, which results the success of crowdfunding. These two components advance the scale effect of crowdfunding and realize the straight climb of the industry.

Another crowdfunding's feature is lower costs, which is also benefited from the modern technology- big data technology. Crowdfunding's advantages in the information gathering, high-speed information analyzing and automatic information processing reduce cost efficiently. Simultaneously it profits from advantages such as simplicity of understanding and using, flexibility of accessing, high comfort level, perpetual improvement in customer experiences etc.

Source: Blog: Crowdfunding Arab Based Platforms[22]

[22] Blog< http://ahmadsb.com/crowdfunding-arab-based-platforms/>, date of access: 02.12.2015

In last five years, equity and debt based crowdfunding platforms show an upward trend. Crowdfunding becomes an alternative form of start-ups financing. In the pioneering period of start-ups, entrepreneurs often do not have guarantee for their financing, therefore the initial investment is very risky, financial institutions e.g. banks usually reject their debt applications. Risky businesses can be only financed by angel investors or venture capitalists, but private equities have an extremely high rate of rejection. Equity or debt crowdfunding become an alternative, as some as the private equity, they involve in many kinds of risks. In order to reduce them for investors, crowdfunding platforms have implemented diverse risk management approaches and provide various risk management instruments. This book deeply analyses the risk management in crowdfunding in the fourth chapter.

**Chapter 2.1.1 - Crowdfunding Actors**

In crowdfunding, there are several characters. Generally, we classify them into initiator, funders and intermediary- platforms.

- Initiator

Initiators are individuals or organizations, who use crowdfunding mechanisms, promote business ideas or projects, offer investment opportunities, and request „direct access to the market and simultaneously gather financial support from truly interested supporters"[23]. In many literatures, initiators are substituted with „entrepreneurs ", based on their large proportion.

- Funder

Funders of crowdfunding are individuals, who network and pool their money together to finance the business ideas and projects. Depending on different crowdfunding models, funders expect a related payoff, which can be paid in form of rewards, company shares, loan interests or other return. Compare to the traditional investment, crowdfunding investment shows up the key difference to individual investor, that funders actively select and decide for projects

[23] cf. Ordanini et al. 2013: 5

directly, the investment amount is used to be smaller.

- Platforms

Indeed of personal networks, crowdfunding platforms play a role as organizational coordinator. Through the platform, initiators and funders meet each other. Initiators propose their business idea or projects on the platform, funders build up a „crowd" to finance together through the platform. Some platforms have built an investor alliance since founding.

Generally, platforms are absorbed for one or a few business fields, and they are specialized for a certain funding model. Crowdfunding for musicians e.g. ArtisteConnect supports local artists[24], the crowdfunding platform links artists direct with their fans, not only from the market perspective, but also in terms of financing. Fans can contribute funds to their favorite musicians, if the financing target has been reached, artists are allowed to use the fund to produce CDs etc. Famous platforms such as Indiegogo and Kickstarter appear since 2008, "who changed the way grassroots filmmakers approach the public for funding"[25], emphasize creation and innovation, have become most popular crowdfunding platforms worldwide. AngelList and Early Shares are most successful equity crowdfunding platforms, both are U.S. based, focus on raising equity for start-up companies and small business, which involve in a high degree of risks. AngelList even only accept accredited investors to ensure the risk taking ability of their investors.

Even though crowdfunding platforms provide service in the same business field, there are obvious differences in funding models, preference of projects etc.

The agency fee and services charges of platforms have various pricing mechanisms and payment modes. The reward crowdfunding platform Kickstarter charges 5% of raised funds for successful projects, if the target is not reached,

---

[24] ArtisteConnect <http://www.artisteconnect.com/about>, date of access: 02.08.2014

[25] Pozin 2012: <http://www.forbes.com/sites/ilyapozin/2012/12/20/crowdfunding-the-future-of-the-film-industry/ >, date of access: 02.08.2014

there is no fees to pay[26]; the equity based crowdfunding platform MicroVentures asks $100 for submitting an application to get into the initial screening, $250 for due diligence, MicroVentures charges 5% of total funds from the initiator and 5% from the funder if the raising is successful, additionally investors pay 10% carry interest[27]; reward based crowdfunding platform Indiegogo takes 9% fee on the raised fund if the target amount is not reached, 4% fee if the raising goal is reached[28]; the debt based crowdfunding Bettervest charges 10% of raised capital if the raising is successful, an annual handling fee of 1% has to be paid by initiators[29]; one of the largest crowdfunding platform YouCaring offers their services for free, no initiators have been charged[30].

Another observed phenomenon is that, working processes of different crowdfunding platforms are less varietal, but their services vary greatly. Although every platform has different business ideas, the quality of service, the sense of responsibility, the level of expertise influences the platforms' reputation, impact their ranking in the market, and also play a decisive role in promoting this young industry.

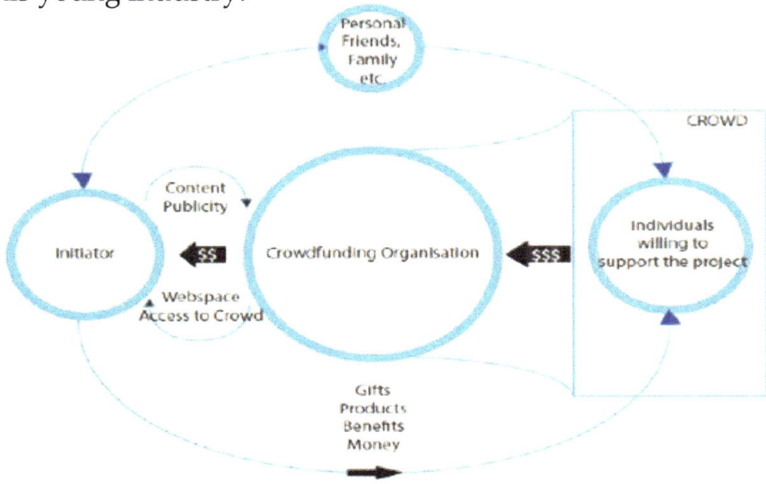


Source:
Grin: Online Crowdfunding in Turkey

26 Kickstarter <https://www.kickstarter.com>, date of access: 02.08.2014

27 MicroVentures Interview< http://www.thecrowdcafe.com/microventures-snapshot/>, date of access: 02.08.2014

28 Indiegogo <https://go.indiegogo.com/pricing-fees>, date of access: 02.08.2014

29 Bettervest< https://bettervest.de/de/content/faq/>, date of access: 02.08.2014

30 Youcaring <http://www.youcaring.com/fees>, date of access: 02.08.2014

Instead of concentrating their investments, funders diversify their investment portfolio through the access to many projects via platform. Unlike traditional agencies, these platforms ask for no (or low) management fees and carried interest. The platforms cut the operating cost themselves by enlarging the projects line.

### Chapter 2.1.2 - Crowdfunding Process

In order to explain crowdfunding's funding process, we divide the whole process into eight steps.

- First step: Identification of users' requirement

From the initiators' perspective, before submitting an application, initiators have to learn their own requirements. Crowdfunding is an approach to raise fund, but not the process of producing ideas. A vague application may barely be rejected by platforms, and it can hardly attract funders. In the first step, initiators consider the goal of their funding, business plan, product plan, target amount, before they continue with the second step.

From the funders' aspect, the first step is also the most important one. Before any investment activities, funders need to know own motivations, needs, ability, experience and financial state. Sophisticated investors or professional angel investors have totally different expectations for their investment than inexperience funders, motivations of joining crowdfunding investment may be very individual. Understanding own demands helps funders to target specific crowdfunding platforms and projects.

- Second step: Selection of platforms

There are several thousand crowdfunding platforms, some of them operate globally, some of them focus on the domestic market, most of platforms have single crowdfunding model, a few have fixed models, some charge a high fee, some offer service for free, some platforms are specialized for niche businesses, some have a wide scale of business. Every platform has own characteristics, professional fields and advantages. The reputation also plays a big role. Both initiators and funders need to research platforms and choose the most suitable one to meet their own requirements.

- Third step: Submitting an application

From the initiators' perspective, once a platform is chosen, initiators may submit a pitch application introduce the platform investment opportunities they offer and the funding amount they expect. Every platform requires different information and documents according to the form of business. Equity or debt based crowdfunding platforms have strict requirements. Once the application is proven, initiators are allowed to create their campaigns.

From the funders' perspective, some platforms especially equity crowdfunding platforms only allow sophisticated investors or accredited investors to invest according to the regulation. Funders are also asked to submit some relative documents, and pass the test of risk awareness. After the investors' valuation, qualified funders are allowed to open their investment account and set their portfolio.

During this step, most of platforms pre-screen projects and do the background check. Some platforms require third party valuation; some do due diligence themselves. A few platforms such as the Chinese platform Angelcrunch offer additional service and support with business plans. For some brilliant ideas with incompetent business plans, platforms reject the initial application and help with improvement.

- Fourth step: Creating the campaign

Initiators get an own project page to create campaigns, the campaign is a part of the marketing plan. Beside the text and pictorial introduction of opportunity, financial projection, they normally add videos, third party reference. Crowdfunding platforms focus much on educating their users to create a successful campaign. The target amount has also to be published in the project page, some platforms have flexible funding model, which means if the funding goal is not reached, initiators still have access to the raised fund, some platforms offer fixed funding, meaning if the target is not reached, the funding project fails. Another component is the duration, which gives a time period for fund raising activities. Payoff for funders is also important to be point out. In the donation based crowdfunding, funders get nothing or rewards, in the equity crowdfunding, funders act as shareholders and get shares of the company, debt crowdfunding promises interest payoff and repayment after maturity.

- Fifth step: Activation of campaign

Once the campaign is online, it comes into the activation period. Funders are able to view campaigns, ask questions and make decision. In the fifth step, platforms are actively involved, many platforms enable the communication between initiators and funders, arrange meetings, promote projects etc. The investments are accumulated until the funding goal is reached or till the end of the duration. Funders may use the time to request more information, or communicate with different participants, enable to decide, if invest or not, and much to invest.

- Sixth step: Completing fund raising

Once the duration runs out, campaigns are executed. In the fixed finance model, if the target is hit, the project gets funded, if the goal is not reached, the project fails, initiators do not have access to already raised capital, funders loose the opportunity to invest. In the flexible finance model, initiators receive whatever they raise via campaigns. After fund raising, investors are required to confirm their willing of joining, some platforms offer a so-called „cooling period" for reconsideration. After the period runs out, the investment becomes a binding order.

- Seventh Step: Executing the funding

After previous six steps, funding is executed. With strong involvement of platforms, initiators are requested to prepare for the execution, including the completion of legal documents, shareholder's agreement (in equity crowdfunding) etc. Also funders are required to be background checked, in order to ensure, that there is no suspicion of money laundering and other illegal intention, every party is protected. After the completion of preparation, the fund is transferred from funders to initiators.

For successful projects, initiators are charged fee from platforms, which can be more than 10% and also can be free.

- Eighth Step: Issuing share certifications and other operational steps
- For the equity crowdfunding, there are more steps, initiators calculate the number of shares to be issued and the dilution of existing shares. New share certificates need to be issued promptly. A few equity crowdfunding platforms and debt crowdfunding platforms with venture capital funds' characteristics also involve in hinder operation.

**Exhibit 2. Crowdfunding Process**

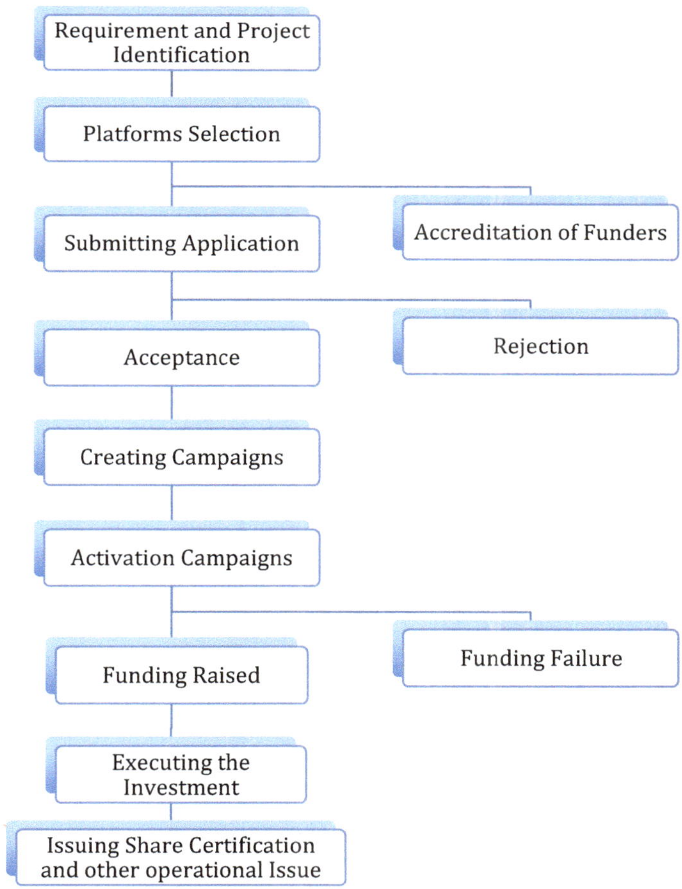

### Chapter 2.1.3 - Crowdfunding Models

In the sphere of academy, the classification of crowdfunding models has many possibilities such as using the time period of funding to define models, using return for investments to define models[31] etc. According to the mainstream opinion and major literatures, crowdfunding is structured into non-profit crowdfunding models such as „donation crowdfunding", „reward crowdfunding", and models with financial payoff „debt crowdfunding" and „equity crowdfunding"[32].

- Donation based crowdfunding:

Donation based funding is the root of other models, it refers the charity via online channels such as crowdfunding platforms. Compare to other models, funders in donation-based crowdfunding do not expect any return in any form for their contribution. Although the reward-based crowdfunding also does not allow financial return, but rewards are promised. Donation crowdfunding is often used by non-profit organizations and their social activities. Causevox is one representative of donation-based crowdfunding, which targets non-profit social projects. Another example is Razoo, a US-based platform, which focuses on animal protection and other social good projects.

- Reward based crowdfunding:

Reward based crowdfunding is the most popular model of crowdfunding, it has acquired many success-stories. It is often used to finance small businesses, creative ideas, cultural projects, technological experiments, low-cost product development. As same as donation-based crowdfunding, reward crowdfunding does not offer any monetary return, but investors get a non-monetary reward.

In this Model, funders finance collaboratively in return of a material or immaterial reward. The quality and quantity of rewards are related to the amount of financing. The most well-known case was the political funding of Obama in 2008, funders are promised to join dinner with George Clooney. The globally

[31] cf.Röthler, Wenzlaff 2011: 12
[32] cf Rossi 2014: 6

operated platforms Kickstarter and Indiegogo are both reward based. Kickstarter focuses on financing creative ideas and projects, Indiegogo has a flexible funding mode, more projects and businesses are accepted, initiators have access to the raised fund, even if the target amount is not reached. Funders in Indiegogo expect to be repaid with rewards three months after funding activities.

- Debt based crowdfunding:

Debt based crowdfunding develops rapidly in the North America, it is sometimes obscure with P2P lending. For some reasons, initiators are not able to acquire loans from traditional financial institutes, debt crowdfunding is an alternative way to raise fund for financial needs. Initiators request a specific amount of loan, a numinous of funders give a loan in return for interest. The repayment of total borrowed amount muss be promised. Compare to donation-based crowdfunding and equity-based crowdfunding, debt crowdfunding faces more credit risk and market risk.

- Equity based crowdfunding:

Equity based crowdfunding is another rising star of crowdfunding. It's used by companies such as start-ups, SMEs. Initiators e.g. entrepreneurs seek capital for new businesses or small businesses, a numinous of funders finance them together in exchange of companies' shares, investors expect a long-term return on their equity investment. The repayment of total investment is not guaranteed, but funders obtain ownership and expect potential financial successes. This model is deeply concerned by regulators, JOBS in the U.S., FCA in the UK both regulate the equity crowdfunding investment.

In order to analyze the research theme „risk management in crowdfunding", the object of study is focused on models with financial return, which are debt-based crowdfunding and equity-based crowdfunding.

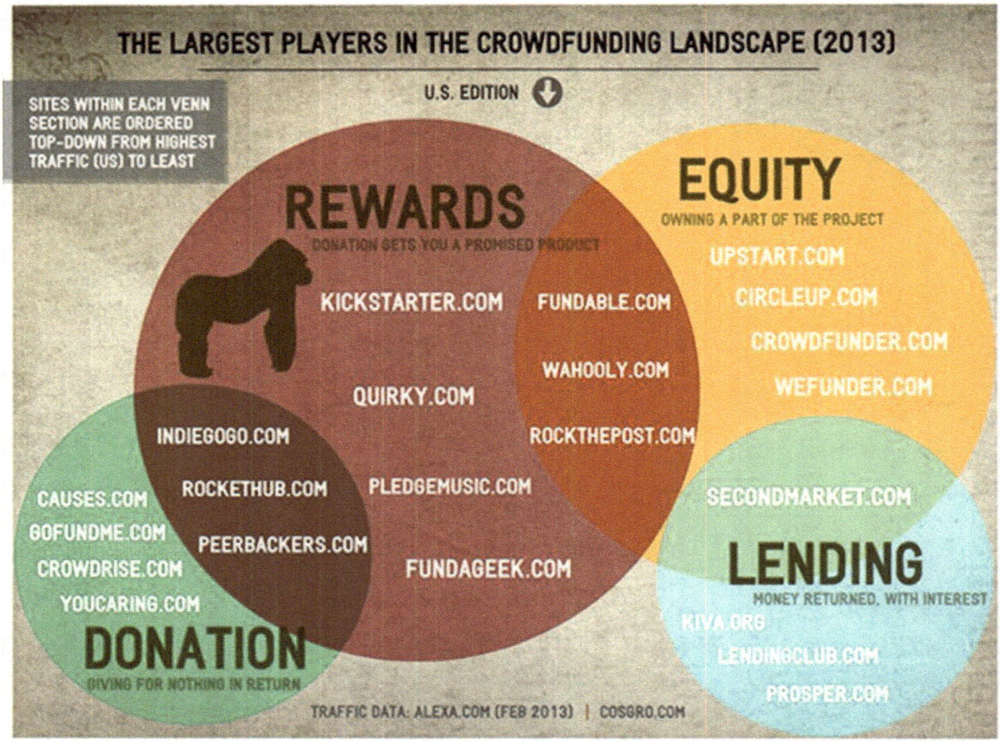


Source: Alexa.com[33]

[33]Alexa.com <http://www.jamieburke.co.uk/wp-content/uploads/2014/04/Top-Crowdfunding-Sites-US_2013_tmb.jpg > date of access: 02.12.2015

## Chapter 2.2 - History and Development

Although the basic concept of crowdfunding has hundreds years' history, even Mozart and Beethoven have financed their concerts with fundraising through the community, but online crowdfunding is still in the infancy.

Looking back at the history, we notice the impact of art-industry, early activities are mainly connected with art: In 1997, the British rock band Marillion raised $60,000 from its fans to finance an U.S. tour, the funding was organized by fans without any involvement of financial institutions. It used to be seen as a representative of the crowdfunding in the early stage.

The ArtistShare was launched in October 2003, helps musicals raise money from their fans, and is looked as the first online crowdfunding platform[34][35]. Artists promote and propose their new production ideas, a number of fans finance the production together. Another milestone of crowdfunding implementation appears in politics. During the presidential election in 2008, US president Barack Obama firstly used crowdfunding and raised $750 million from donors, he utilized a crowdfunding strategy to target large groups of small donors. Before 2008, political campaigns are traditionally financed by small groups of wealthy donors. Four years later, Obama replicated the same strategy and raised an amount as double as his rival Mitt Romney. The evidence proofs the crowdfunding's influence in political elections, Obama becomes America's first African-American president and he is re-elected in 2012.

In May 2012, US president Barack Obama signed the Jumpstart Our Business Start-ups Act (JOBS), which proposed the regulatory framework for the public offering through crowdfunding. JOBS paved the way to equity-based crowdfunding and the industry faces a huge opportunity to grow.

Since the emergence of the first online platform ArtistShare, crowdfunding industry celebrated its decade. There is a big increase in number of platforms. According to estimates, there were over 500 active crowdfunding platforms in

---

[34] cf. Freedman/Nutting 2014:

[35] cf. Wharton 2010: <http://knowledge.wharton.upenn.edu/article/can-you-spare-a-quarter-crowdfunding-sites-turn-fans-into-patrons-of-the-arts/ >, date of access: 02.08.2014

the US and Europe[36], and more than 800 registered crowdfunding related domain in China.[37] By the end of 2011, Europe raised €300 million, considering all types of crowdfunding, and there were 200 active crowdfunding platforms[38]. The Crowdfunding Industry Report by Massolution presents: the crowdfunding industry has globally raised $2.7 billion in 2012 and across more than 1 million individual campaigns[39]. Although the result of 2014 is still not available, but crowdfunding is expected to provide $65 billion to the global economy in 2014[40]. The World Bank commissioned study predicts a $93 billion equivalent crowdfunding investing market by 2025, and crowdfunding is truly global[41].

---

[36] cf. Caldbeck 2013: <http://www.forbes.com/sites/ryancaldbeck/2013/06/23/crowdfunding-trends-which-crowdfunding-sites-will-survive/>, date of access: 02.08.2014
[37] cf. Liu/Luo 2014: 29, translated by the author
[38] cf. De Buysere et al. 2012: ??
[39] cf. Massolution: 7
[40] Clifford <http://www.entrepreneur.com/article/230912>, date of access: 02.08.2014
[41] cf. Swart <http://www.pbs.org/mediashift/2013/12/world-bank-crowdfunding-investment-market-to-hit-93-billion-by-2025/>, date of access: 02.08.2014

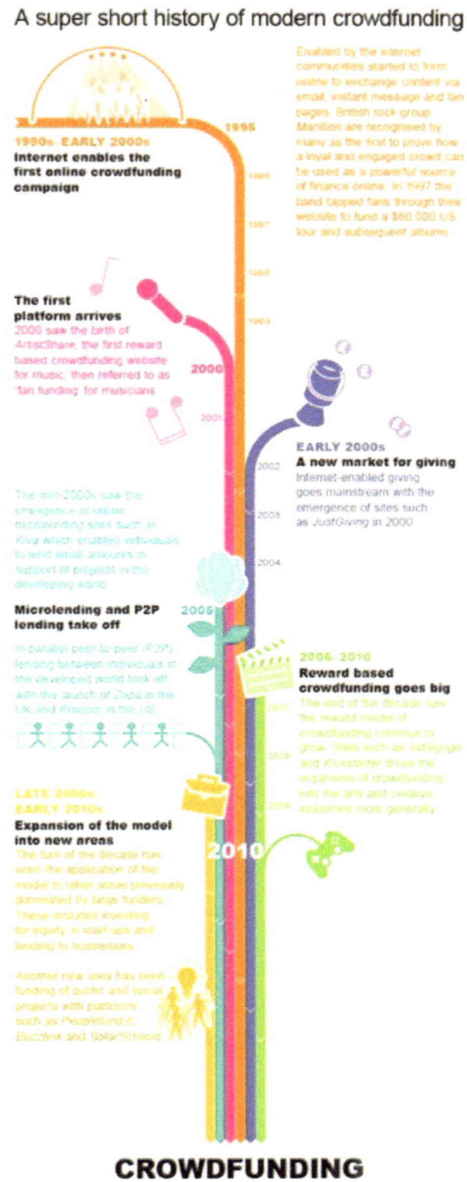


Source: Nesta: News and Features[42]

[42] Nesta<http://www.nesta.org.uk/news/history-crowdfunding>, date of access: 02.12.2015

## Chapter 2.3 - Regulation

During the crowdfunding industry grows rapidly, national and local legislators pay significant attentions, establish regulatory framework to maintain the sustainable development. This chapter introduces some existing policies and regulations, outline a number of potential development.

In the dynamic financial market, regulation often lags behind the market development. As a new financial instrument, crowdfunding challenges policy makers. The current status shows that most of countries still do not implement any specific legislations, which may hinder the industrial continued development in the global context.

Currently various countries seize the time to implement researches and work on drafts, they mainly focus on the investor protection, therefor the donation based crowdfunding and the reward based crowdfunding are not subject to supervision, in which investors do not expect financial return. The regulation of debt-based crowdfunding is on the national base. For example UK requires debt based crowdfunding platforms to be authorized by Financial Conduct Authority (FCA) as same as equity crowdfunding platforms, Germany only requires a straightforward license under der German Trade, Commerce and Industry Regulation Act[43].

The equity crowdfunding attracts more regulatory attention based on its characteristics like a financial service provider. In the US, Jumpstart Our Business Start-ups Act (JOBS) lays a foundation of legitimacy of equity crowdfunding, it provides an initial regulatory framework, pass to the Securities and Exchange Commission (SEC). „JOBS is designed to ease restrictions on capital-raising across a broad spectrum of finance“[44], it has proposed a line of rules for equity crowdfunding, such as equity crowdfunding platforms must register as a broker or „funding portal“, crowdfunding must file a disclosure document with the SEC, crowdfunding is not allowed to advertise in public, crowdfunding funders are only allowed to invest less than 10% of annual income or net

---

43 European Crowdfundfunding Network 2013: 11

44 Forbes <http://www.forbes.com/sites/deborahljacobs/2013/10/23/sec-proposes-crowdfunding-rules/>, date of access: 02.08.2014

worth. The JOBS Act is remarked as impractical from many industrial insiders. According to the published information, the SEC intents to finalized the proposed rules in October 2015. How it goes, is still unclear.

Source: Crowdfunder :News[45]

The European Commission generally supports the development of crowdfunding and has issued the Communication, „Unleashing the potential of crowdfunding in the European Union" in March 2014[46]. For the regulation of crowdfunding, European Commission proposed a rough framework, each country is responsible for the legislation and the supervision. According to the European Crowdfunding Network, platforms in UK are required by the Financial Services and Markets Act 2000 to be authorized by the independent economic regulator for payment systems Financial Conduct Authority (FCA). „However, seeking authorization is a costly and time-consuming process and obliges the regulated firm to comply with the FCA's conduct of business obli-

---

45 Crowdfunder< https://www.crowdfunder.com/blog/category/jobs-act/ >, date of access: 02.12.2015

46 European Commission <http://ec.europa.eu/internal_market/finances/docs/crowdfunding/140327-communication_en.pdf>, date of access: 02.08.2014

gations to ensure that the investments arranged through the platform are appropriate for the investor on a case-by-case basis"[47]. FCA requires that involved risks should be highlighted and the capital reserves against the extreme events have to be taken in consideration. FCA only allows sophisticated or accredited funders to invest via crowdfunding. The rules stipulate that, funders with rich investment experience, high net worth or investing maximum 10% of their net investable assets are able to invest via crowdfunding. The investors are also required to pass the appropriateness test to prove their awareness of risks.

In Germany, equity crowdfunding platforms are required with the written license from the German Financial Supervisory Authority (German: Bundesanstalt für Finanzdienstleistungsaufsicht, BaFin) based on their behavior of offering securities. But according to the article „Crowdfunding and supervisory law "from September 2012, BaFin allows platforms, which only offer interests in silent partnership, to benefit from a statutory exception to the licensing requirement. In November 2014, the German federal government has published the revised draft of the German Retail Investors' Protection Act (Kleinanlegerschutzgesetz), it provides for further restriction and take individual need of crowdfunding into account. It limits the maximum investment amount of one funder in one project to €1.000, if the funder invests more than €1.000, the regulator requires cash deposit for financial instrument, €10.000 is set as the absolute maximum investment amount for one investor per project, € 1 million is the maximum total investment of one funder. The main critics focus on that, there is no special treatment for sophisticated investors. The draft is not yet adopted by the Federal Council and the law will be expected to enter into force by mid-2015 at earliest[48].

China is regarded as an attractive market for crowdfunding with the biggest growth potential in Asia, the market is forecasted with $50 billion worth in the

---

47 European Crowfunding Network 2013: 19

48 German Crowdfunding Network <http://www.germancrowdfunding.net/2014/11/government-draft-of-german-crowdfunding-regulation-retail-investors-protection-act-kleinanlegerschutzgesetz/ >, date of access: 30.01.2015

next decade[49]. Like in the other financial services' area, China's lack of regulation appears in the Internet-based finance industry. For equity crowdfunding or debt-based crowdfunding, China Securities Regulatory Commission (CSRC) has not yet passed any legislation or laws. On 18th. December 2014, Securities Association of China (Chinese: 中国证券业协会 SAC) published a trial draft of the Equity Crowdfunding Regulation Act (Chinese:私募股权众筹融资管理办法(试行)(征求意见稿)), after receiving numerous critics, SAC revises the initial draft on 31st. January 2015. As similar as the draft from Germany, the SAC stipulates that only investors, who can comply the conditions may invest in equity crowdfunding, funders need to confirm with either ¥500.000 annual income in the last three years or ¥1 million net worth. But in China, only individuals or institutional investors are allowed to invest in crowdfunding, if the minimum investment amount in one project is over ¥100.000. Another component is that, each proven project cannot raise money from over 200 shareholders. The SAC draft sets a high threshold for both initiators and investors.

Regulations are required to advance the development of crowdfunding industry on one hand, and to prevent financial risks on the other hand. Lack of regulation in crowdfunding is a global issue, we could see the difficulty for regulators, that SEC does still not finalize the crowdfunding rules three years after JOBS has been signed.

---

[49] cf. Drake <http://www.entrepreneur.com/article/241389>, date of access: 31.01.2015

# Chapter 3 - Risk Management Theory

In order to analyze the risk management in crowdfunding, the third chapter elaborates the basic theory of risk management in the financial industry, and the fourth chapter explores the characteristics of risk management in the new funding model- Internet based crowdfunding.

The main purpose of the financial market is to allocate capital, to bring saving to loans. All financial activities are return-driven, the market has various kinds of uncertainties and is fraught with different categories of risks, which bring both threats and opportunities. "The greater the risks taken, the higher the return that can be realized"[50].

Theoretically, we define risk as the potential of losing value, or a situation involving exposure to danger[51]. Financial risks are considered as a group of possibilities that shareholders may lose money for their investment, which are caused by strategic decisions, uncertain market developments, operational processes, changes in the legal environment and regulation, inaccurate credit assessment, natural disaster etc. In the modern theory, the standard deviation or variance of a portfolio is used to define risks[52]. The risk management is a way to prevent losses, it has the purpose to minimize, monitor and control the downside and achieve positive return.

---

[50] Hull 2012: 2

[51] Oxford Dictionaries: < http://www.oxforddictionaries.com/definition/english/risk>, date of access: 19.01.2015

[52] Wikipedia: < http://en.wikipedia.org/wiki/Financial_risk>, date of access: 19.01.2015

Source: Kintetsu World Express: KWE Group Risk Management Policy[53]

[53] Kintetsu World Express< http://www.kweaus.com/kwe-group-risk-management-policy/>, date of access： 02.12.2015

## Chapter 3.1 - The Concept of Risk Management

Risk management has significant meaning for the continual development of financial industry. The prudent risk management reduces the injury of unexpected events, help the planning and the decision-making.

The risk management is a process of identification, assessment, treatment and controlling to manage uncertainties with negative consequences. The effective process improves the viability, the competitiveness, the sustainable development, the preparation for changes and undesirable out-coming, and the better resources allocation.

In many financial institutions such as banks, asset management firms and insurance companies, risk management is their daily work, professional skills and technologies are their core assets, the ability of dealing with risks influences their performances, and is the key factor determining the outcome of financial activities.

Risk management should not be confused with the risk taking, and it is not a part of the risk taking process. Risk management uses the maximum risk taking capacity to calculate the limit for risk exposures.

In 2009, the International Organization for Standardization codifies the standards, methodologies and processes and provides principle on risk management, which is named ISO 31000[54].

---

[54] ISO <http://www.iso.org/iso/home/standards/iso31000.htm>, date of access: 19.01.2015

## Chapter 3.2 - Risk Management Process

According to the ISO3000, the risk management process has following steps:

In this process, first two steps- identification and measurement are applied to provide data for developing the risk management strategy and its implementation.

### Chapter 3.2.1 - Identification of Risks

Being able to control the downside, it is necessary to understand risks themselves. Identification is the first step in the risk management process, which contributes the foundation of establishing an effective strategy.

There are several methods to identify risks such as scenario analysis. The scenario analysis bases on internal and external data sources, and forecast possible future events and their out comings. For example, changes in economic environment, instabilities of political situation, new regulations or legislations etc are taken in the consideration. Having different perspectives is critical in the scenario analysis, that risks can be considered in full-scale.

There are a number of risk types occurring in the finance, some are common to other businesses, and some are specific in the financial industry. The main types of financial risks are introduced compendiously.

- Credit risk

The credit risk refers to default of promised cash flows. It appears in various situations, e.g. borrowers default on debt by failing to pay interests and repayment. The sovereign risk refers that government bond issuers are not able to pay the coupon or repay bonds, the companies fail to make payments for invoices etc. This is the main risk for lenders.

- Market risk

The financial market develops rapidly, the market risk is referred to consequences of future market's uncertainty, is the risk of losses in position arising from movements in market prices[55]. The volatile pricing of stocks, the inconstant interest rate, the instable currency rates, or the non-determinacy of the market in the real economy fall within the market risk, which can be predicted by doing numerous researches, predictions can have different periods of time, and they are never guaranteed and 100% accurate.

- Liquidity risk

Liquidity risk describes the probability of potential loss causing by the lack of the ability to trade. If an asset or a security cannot be traded fluidly, it may generate the cost of time, the cost of capital, or reduce the remained earning. The liquidity risk is defined into market liquidity risk and funding liquidity risk.

- Operational risk:

The Basel Committee on Banking Supervision defines the operational risk as „the risk of loss resulting from inadequate or failed internal processes, people and systems, or from external events" and „the capital charge should cover

[55] Wikipedia:< http://en.wikipedia.org/wiki/Market_risk#cite_note-1>, date of access: 20.01.2015

direct as well as certain indirect losses".[56] In 2014, the committee has proposed an improved operational risk capital framework with suggestion on new approaches.

The operational risk is a wide range of different kinds of risks, which occurs during the operation process, it includes the technical risk, the behavioral risk, the legal risk, the political risk etc., the bigger the project, the higher the probability of operational risk occurrence. This category of risks is closely related to the administrative process and operational procedures. The business performance, the reputation and shareholder value are very sensitive to operational risk.

The operational risk has some specific characteristics, which differs from other risk categories: the operational risk does not occur to seek profit and it cannot be completely eliminated. It exists when processes are running. The operational risk cannot be fully avoided, diversified; it is commonly managed with an aside capital reserve.

- Reputational risk

The reputational risk is referred to the potential negative influence of public opinions according to the business practices. Building the reputation takes years, but it can be destroyed quickly and easily, trigger issues for the negative public attention are not even the focal point, the diffusion affects dramatic decline in business result and increasing costs in operation. The reputational risk is categorized side by side with the credit risk, the market risk, the liquidity risk, and the operational risk. Compare with other risk types, the reputational risk is difficult to identify previously, and the loss is hard to quantify. To manage reputational risk, the supported corporate governance is indispensable, organizations need to build strong relationships with customers, guarantee good communications and work out emergency plans.

- Strategic Risk

The strategic risk is defined as uncertainties in business development, which

---

[56] Basel Committee on Banking Supervision: <http://www.bis.org/bcbs/ca/fobken2.pdf>, date of access: 22.01.2015

could result loss from an inappropriate strategic planning, from a hasty decision-making, from an inflexible adjustment ability etc. This risk type is well connected with involved industries, the business environment, and the resources allocation. Strategically mistakes have huge harmful effect, can even threaten companies' subsistence. Managing strategic risk has not only the purpose to avoid the downside, but can also create new values by taking advantages of uncertainty, that is the reason that strategic risk management becomes the high priority in many companies and is executed by the management team. Enable to analyze strategic risk, many institutions apply their own intelligence models and intergrade models into their strategic planning processes.

Source: Allianz Global Corporate& Specialty[57]

[57] : Allianz Global Corporate& Specialty<http://www.agcs.allianz.com/assets/Graphics/Risk%20Barometer%202013/Allianz%20Business%20risks%202013%20underestimate%20risks.jpg >,date of access: 02.12.2015

## Chapter 3.2.2 - Risk Measurement

After recognizing the risk type, it is necessary to estimate their consequences, in order to decide for an adequate risk management strategy and relative instruments. The measurement obtains the prediction, which is never completely accurate. Financial institutions use the assessment to determine the amount of reserve asset[58], to make the risk taking ability acceptable to regulators. There are many ways to implement the measurement. The most well-known measures are introduced selectively.

- Credit scoring models

Credit risk evaluation becomes very sophisticated at the present age. For financial institutions, especially commercial banks, debt and credit are their core businesses, credit scoring models are widely used to determine the borrowers' credit rating. There are several similar models e.g. linear probability models, logit models etc. The scoring calculation is based on the plenty of information such as the payment records, the amount of debt, the quantity of credit cards etc. Scores range from poorest 300 to the top 850, they show directly the volume of the credit risk. The higher the scores, the lower the credit risk, and vice versa. These scores do not only effect the lender's decision but are also used to price the interest, higher credit scores allow borrowers get better conditions and lower interest rates.

- Third party rating

The availability, the quality and costs of information are critical factors in the credit assessment[59]. Funders either develop their own models to assess the borrower's credit or use the paid third party service to estimate the credit risk and make the appropriate strategic plan.

The credit rating for governments and companies, the market risk assessment, the business model related risk evaluation etc., are often provided by rating agencies like Moody's, Standard & Poor's, Fitch Rating. Lenders pay a fee to get the third-parties' forecasts about the insolvency possibility, the bankruptcy

---

[58] Wikipedia: <http://en.wikipedia.org/wiki/Risk_measure>, date of access: 20.01.2015
[59] Urbanek 2013: 13

possibility or the credit evaluation based on objective analyses and independent assessments. These rating agencies have incredible impacts on the market, they can even cause big changes in the value debt. In most cases, creditors request rating agencies to carry out investigations for own debt issues and seek a credit rating for themselves. The credit rating for private borrowers is provided by credit reporting agencies such as Equifax, TransUnion.

- The Value at Risk (VaR)

The Value at Risk (VaR) is the most widely used risk measures. Under the normal market condition, VaR is widely used to estimate the market risk and the interest rate risk, it gives the maximum loss at a given confidence level over a fixed time horizon, but it cannot determine losses in extreme events. By summarizing the distribution of potential losses (or gain) and pointing out the frontier of bigger losses, users are able to establish risk management strategies. The commonly used probabilities in VaR are 1% and 5%, which means that, there are only 1% or 5% probabilities of losing more than VaR. Time horizons can vary from one day to 1 year. There are three approaches to calculate VaR: Historic or Back Simulation, Variance approach, and Monte Carlo Simulation.

The Historic Simulation assumes that the future risk development stays the same as in the history, it uses as much as possible historical data of return and reorganizes them into the order from worst to best, and then take out the lowest 1% or 5%, which show the losses of worst historical records, VaR with 1% or 5% confidence are easily found out.

The Variance approach assumes that returns are normally distributed. The calculation only requests an expected return and an estimated standard deviation to draw a normal distribution curve, the data at 1% or 5% can be shown easily.

The Monte Carlo Simulation was named in the 20th century, but its basic theory has appeared since 18th century in the Buffon's Needle. It refers to model developing which randomly generates multiple hypothetical trials. The result of randomly trials is ordered from worst to best. The worst 1% or 5% show the possibility of extreme events and helps for decision-making.

## Exhibit 3. Three approaches to calculate VaR

Graph: Historical Method: the distribution of the historical returns[60]

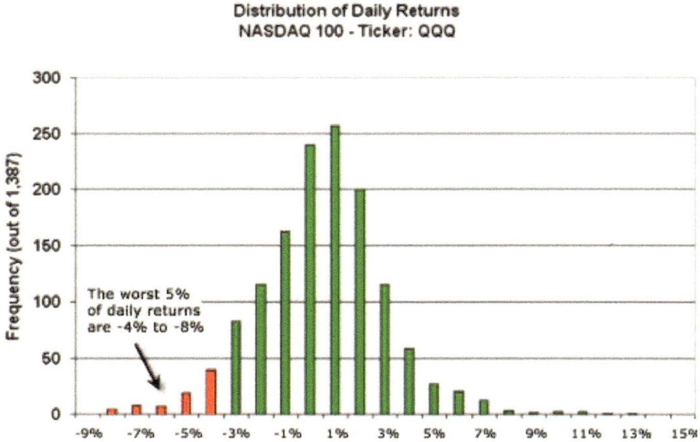


Graph: Variance-Covariance Method: the distribution of the historical returns vs. a normal distribution[61]

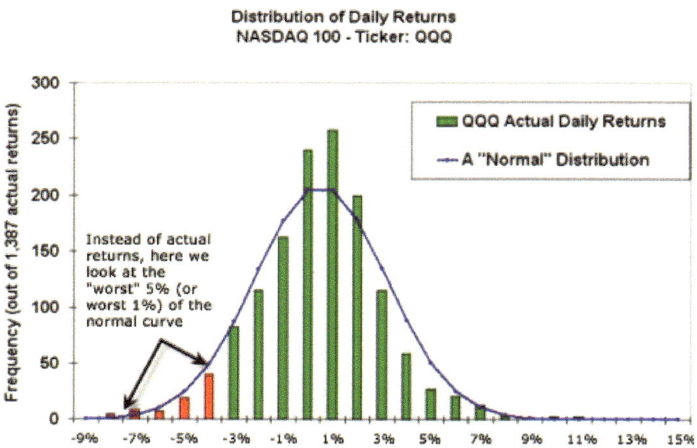


60 Investopedia:<http://www.investopedia.com/articles/04/092904.asp>, date of access: 20.01.2015

61 Investopedia:<http://www.investopedia.com/articles/04/092904.asp>, date of access: 20.01.2015

Graph: Monte Carlo Simulation: the distribution of the historical volatility of QQQ[62]

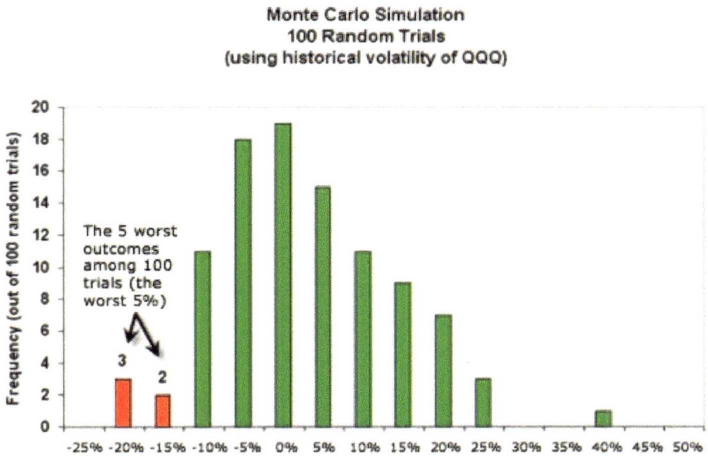


The liquidity-adjusted VaR enable to measure the liquidity risk, which adds the exogenous liquidity cost (ELC) to the VaR. Enable to calculate the ELC, the worst expected half-spread at a particular confidence level is used[63].

- Variance and Volatility

In statistics, Variance is used for probability distribution. It measures the spread of each number to the mean, and it leads to the volatility (standard deviation) determination. A large variance indicates that, individual numbers are far away from the mean, a large volatility shows that, returns rise or fall drastically in a short time period. A high volatility is considered as high risk, because the return fluctuates widely between negative and positive in a short

62 Investopedia:<http://www.investopedia.com/articles/04/092904.asp>, date of access: 20.01.2015

63 cf. Bervas 2006: 69

time period. The following formulas are used for calculation:

Variance : $$\sigma^2 = \frac{\sum(X-\mu)^2}{n}$$

$(X-\mu)$ ...Difference between number and the mean

n... number of values

Volatility: $$\sigma = \sqrt{\sigma^2}$$

The volatility is calculated on the historical data, it does not offer a guarantee for future stability, but it is effective for comparison of different projects with similar investment strategy and expected returns. Lower volatility means maximum return received for the acquired risk.

- Liquidity Gap

The liquidity gap is a simply approach to measure liquidity risk. It describes the difference between liquid assets and the total liabilities[64]. The result can be positive or negative, a negative gap means that there is no net liquid assets left over after fulfilment of liabilities.

- Bid-ask spread

The bid-offer spread is used to measure liquidity and the cost of liquidity, it's often used in the financial trading business. This index assumes that, the transaction is able to happen at any time immediately, the transaction cost is able to be paid in any cases[65]. The bid-ask spread is calculated with a simple formulary:

$$\frac{offer - bid}{offer} \times 100\%$$

- Basic indicator approach

The basic indicator approach is proposed by the Basel Committee on Banking

[64] Investopedia : <http://www.investopedia.com/terms/l/liquidity-gap.asp>, date of access: 22.01.2015
[65] cf. Bervas 2006: 68

Supervision, who proposed several techniques approaches to measure the operational risk, the basic indicator approach is the most simply one. According to the proposer, institutions have to hold capital for operational risk equal to the 15% of average of positive annual gross income over the previous three years[66]. The negative gross income will be excluded.

- Standardized approach

The standardized approach is another method, which is proposed under the Basel capital adequacy. This approach has the same concept as the basic indicator approach, instead of regarding the business as a synthesis, the standardized approach analyses each business line, the capital reserve is calculated separately by multiplying gross income by a Beta factor assigned to that business line[67]. The given Beta factor varies from 12% to 18%.

- Advanced measurement approach

Basel Committee on Banking Supervision proposed the advanced measurement approach as a replenishment to fill the deficiency of other two methods. According to advanced measurement, institutions are allowed to develop their own empirical models to quantify requested reserve capital for operational risk[68], the measure model needs to include more factors such as the scenario analysis, the business environment and internal control etc. The Adoption of advanced measurement approach needs to be approved by regulators.

### Chapter 3.2.3 - Risk Management

In the modern business environment, risk management becomes the major focus in the management level, companies employ analysts to measure risks and integrate risk management into the business strategy and planning processes.

In the third step of risk management process, strategies and approaches are

---

[66] Basel Committee on Banking Supervision: < http://www.bis.org/publ/bcbs118.pdf>, date of access: 22.01.2015

[67] Wikipedia: < http://en.wikipedia.org/wiki/Standardized_approach_(operational_risk)>, date of access: 22.01.2015

[68] cf. Wikipedia: < http://en.wikipedia.org/wiki/Standardized_approach_(operational_risk)>, date of access: 22.01.2015

decided based on the understanding for potential risks and securable resources. The fully functioning of risk management process has to be secured by a compatible organization-structure, and be driven by boards and the management team. Risk avoidance, risk transfer, diversification and limitation are the main management strategies.

Source: I.P.A: Risk Management[69]

[69] I.P.A.< http://ipaadvisory.com/risk-management>, date of access： 02.12.2015

- Risk Avoidance

The risk avoidance is a risk adverse strategy. After diligent research and analyses for business models, environments, products, the market potential, competition strategies, credit rating etc., decisions are made meticulously. Selecting carefully, rejecting risky applications and tightening financing amount are efficient methods to prevent risk.

- Risk Sharing

Risk Sharing is a common strategy to hedge risks, in which risks transferred to a third party or other parties. There are many possibilities to shift risks e.g. purchasing insurance, security or guarantees of third parties, taking position in options, futures.

Some derivatives have similar functions as insurance e.g. credit default Swap, which is an agreement between sellers and buyers, sellers compensate in case of default, buyers pay a relative fee and get the guarantee for payoff if the loan defaults. Another derivative is the foreign exchange Swap, which is used by institutions to hedge their foreign exchange balances, as well as currency Swap for the long term horizon.

Requiring physical and financial collaterals is another universal way to manage risks, that the loan is only extended with collaterals or guarantee through warrantors.

- Risk diversification

Enable to manage the concentration of risks, which is caused by investing in single or a small number of projects. Diversification is an effective strategy to reduce unsystematic risks by diversifying portfolio, expanding business lines, spreading investments among various projects and markets, investing synergistically.

Diversification is an appropriate approach to manage liquidity risk. Both liquidity supplier and demander can implement this approach to reduce the dependence on a single or a small group of cash flow streams.

- Risk Retention

After the risk measurement, if funders or lenders still decide to make deals, we assume that they take risks consciously and voluntarily. It is significant to adjust the risk taking capacity and build financial reserves. The Basel prescribes capital requirements in order to secure the risk bearing capacity of financial institutions.

The risk adjusted return on capital model is a popular approach to measure the risk-based profitability, it is used to compare different projects with varying risk levels.

$$RAROC = \frac{revenue - expenses - expected\ loss\ +\ capital\ income}{capital}$$

capital income... capital charges* risk-free rate
expected loss... average anticipated loss over the measurement period

To manage the operational risk, regulations especially the Basel demand a minimum capital holding for the operational risk, this reserve is an obligation against loss from operation.

The financial reserve is also an instrument to manage liquidity risk. Based on a scenario analysis, a contingency funding plan is established to prevent sudden liquidity shortage.

### Chapter 3.2.4 - Risk Controlling

The last step in the risk management process is the executing of strategic plans, the monitoring the implementation, the management control, the continuous reporting internally and externally, periodical reviewing and revising of risk management plans. The last step includes a learning process to improve risk management and formalize experience, lessons and information into a reusable form for knowledge sharing and management.

## Chapter 3.3 - Relevance of Risk Management in Crowdfunding

In traditional investment activities, investors' protection is always the primary task of service providers, they use a mass of risk ratios to evaluate the possibility of the downside and use various risk management approaches to hedge risks for investors. As same as in the traditional financial industry, crowdfunding investors also face various kinds of financial risks. Unlike institutional investors and professional angel investors, most of crowdfunding funders do not have specialized knowledge in the risk management. Because of the lack of the risk awareness, the lack of the ability for project valuation, they may be easily influenced by the promised return and creative ideas, and make wrong decisions. This type of funders is much more depended on platforms and their services. Based on the quantity of inexperienced funders, the quality of risk management of platforms directly affects the total investment performance, therefore has a significant meaning.

The fact remains that the lack of regulation exists globally. As we introduced in the 2.3, most important markets (countries) have not yet completed the legislation, crowdfunding may be used for illegal activities, frauds have been discovered in every country. Unlike the traditional investment channels, initiators introduce their business via online campaign pages, they do not need to be personal connected with funders. For some reasons such as geographic distance, funders are not able to investigate projects. All matters increase the probability of the fraud risk. Platforms are not planned for any illegal activities, which destroy the confidence of investors, destroy the reputation of platforms themselves, and question the social security. "How to reduce this risk" becomes a concern for both crowdfunding operators and regulators.

In the investment business, costs of due diligence and credit valuations can hardly be borne by one individual investor, it also makes no sense, that every investor of the same project does the similar research. It causes the waste of resources. Platforms benefit from its ability of information collecting and processing, they are able to carry out an investigation easily.

- The corporate social responsibility is an often spoken area. Crowdfunding platforms are normally companies, based on their form of social network, financial activates and the quantity of funders, platforms have a huge social influence. As intermediaries in the financial industry, platforms gain not only reputation, but also financial success from their effective investors' protection and good risk management.

# Chapter 4 - Risk Management in Crowdfunding

Previous chapters introduce the current state of crowdfunding industry and the basic theory of risk management. In order to answer the research question „Risk Management in Crowdfunding", we focus on requited crowdfunding models, which are debt based crowdfunding and equity based crowdfunding.

The financial industry and the Internet industry both involve in numerous risks, the crowdfunding has characteristics from both businesses. As we analyzed in the second chapter, crowdfunding is used to gather capital from a group of funders, the small amounts are invested collectively. Risks of individuals are diversified or spread out through the synergy, the occurrence of extreme losses is efficiently reduced， the demand for risk hedging is reduced. Compare to traditional financial products, derivatives in crowdfunding are simplified, involved risks are mainly systematic risks. In crowdfunding the risk transfer is still feasible, regulations focus on the behavior supervision and consumer protection.

Crowdfunding benefits from the modern Internet technology, all data can be aggregated effectively, the credit evaluation benefits from the efficiency of the automatic online system, the assessment process becomes quickly, the possibility for human errors is reduced and the cost of information is minimized.

Analyzing the risk management in crowdfunding is relative challenging, because not many researches have been done for this new emerged financing form. In addition to literature search, this research organized numerous case studies and interviews.

## Chapter 4.1 - Involved Risks in Crowdfunding

Traditional risks of financial service still exist in Internet-based crowdfunding, whether it is credit risk, market risk, liquidity risk, operational risk, or other risks. Its potential loss cannot be ignored. The risk management in Crowdfunding focuses the five main risk types: market risk, credit risk, reputational risk, risk of information disclosure and the risk involved in technical security. Last two risks are categorized into operational risk.

- Credit risk in Crowdfunding

The credit risk is mainly connected with the debt crowdfunding model. Although the credit evaluation in the crowdfunding bases on the data integration, the modelling and quantitative analyses, the information asymmetry may still exist. Due to the existence of false information, the manufactured rating etc., the authenticity and the reliability of initial data affect the quality of the credit valuation. Lack of lone-term data accumulation also obsesses some crowdfunding platforms to offer high-quality assessment. Another issue is that, the scientificity and the reliability of measurement models of many platforms are not yet verified. By reason that the supervision and the standardization of the crowdfunding industry are not yet set in many countries. Some platforms only intent to play the role as financing channels, some platforms also act as brokers and warrantors simultaneously, it may possibly result the conflict of interest or the accumulation of risk.

- Liquidity risk in Crowdfunding

As we mentioned in the previous paragraph, crowdfunding chiefly faces systematic risks. In the equity crowdfunding, most of investments are start-ups funding, which involves in high small business risk. The equity crowdfunding has not yet got an efficient marketplace to trade shares, without trading mechanism for crowdfunding securities, the exit is extremely unpredictable and it could take years, the invested amount may be tied up in a long time period. According to the Jumpstart Our Business Start-ups (JOBS) Act, the liquidity risk should be mitigated by limiting of the investment amount[70].

- Reputation risk in Crowdfunding

The reputation risk is a specific risk for organizations, especially in the financial industry, it directly linked to the companies' market value. Crowdfunding platforms have to face the reputational risk at any time. In fact, all platforms are full of enthusiasm about enhancing the funders' profitability to improve their own competitiveness. Some platforms use the high-expected return to attract attention without mechanism for managing correlated risks. It is an effective way to acquire customers and expand the business scale, but once a project cannot achieve the expected return, or even fails, it may trigger the public attention. Also for platforms, which offer more guaranty, if customers are not satisfied with the service during claims, complaints, compensations, and once the process is not handled appropriately, it may easily lead to negative public opinions.

- Operational risk in Crowdfunding

In the crowdfunding environment, the variety of operational risk increases continuously. Compare to the traditional finance, crowdfunding is based on the big data technology, it acquires data automatically via social networks and search engine, all achieved information comes from virtual channels. The authenticity of the information cannot be guaranteed, frauds may exist. This is the biggest issue for the risk management in crowdfunding, and the most challenging part for regulators. As individual funder, it may not easy to do the background check for each project, which is listed on the platform. Reducing the probability of fraudulence is the most important duty for intermediaries, and their ability in this field becomes a competitive strength. The due diligence efficiently reduces the fraud risk, but it may also involve in accrued fees, which can cause the higher transaction cost.

Simultaneously, the risk of fraud can also be begotten by platforms themselves.

---

[70] Cf. U.S. Securities and Exchange Commission, Jumpstart Out Business Startups Act <https://www.sec.gov/spotlight/jobs-act.shtml>, date of access: 22.01.2015

Due to the current regulation, deals do not have to be approved by any regulator, and the transaction information for each deal does not have to be supervised by the third part, the true purpose of transactions, the factual information about invested projects, if there is a conflict of interest or not, cannot be controlled easily. In unmonitored status, funders are very passive. High bankruptcy rate, the involvement in invested projects, the commitment to the unrealistic return etc., may cause by platforms.

Risks of the information disclosure and the privacy protection should not be neglected too. The personal information and the transaction information is collected extensively, the security of this large amount of data is another huge challenge for intermediaries. During the operation, platforms have accesses to funders' sensitive information such as identity documents, contact numbers, bank accounts, the cards' verification code, the validity of credit card etc. The transaction is also executed online; the transaction information is transmitted over the network. During the process of transferring, storage, using and destruction of information, a complete privacy protection mechanism is required, in order to avoid the information leakage. Intermediaries are demanded to own capability to secure the information. January 2014, a big crises of personal data leak broke out in Korea, the personal data of credit card customers were stolen, more than 20 Million of customers became victims, which accounted for one third of the population, and caused a public panic. But compare to traditional financial institutions, many platforms are even more inexperienced, and still endure the risk of information disclosure.

Another operational risk is the technical risk. Crowdfunding relies on the Internet system, it is highly dependent on the computer technology, on the network communication technology and on the trading software. Any deficiency of the network may directly threaten Internet-based financial activities. Another feature of crowdfunding is that, physical characteristics of crowdfunding platforms show great resemblance that, the whole industry can be easily threatened by large- scale attacks. Open system of the communication network, imperfect key management and data encryption, security flaws of TCP/IP protocol, computer viruses, hacker attracts etc., all these threats can lead to a security crisis, and can even become a national security concern. In the traditional financial industry, the technical risk brings limited loss, but in the crowdfunding industry, it is a systematic risk, which can lead to a paralysis of the entire network, can cause a leak of a great mass of data, can lose transaction records and customers, and finally damage the reputation of the whole industry.

Legal risk is also involved in crowdfunding, which is caused by 1) the uncertainty of laws and regulations, 2) the intentional criminality, and 3) the losing of protection for intellectual properties through the public browse.

Crowdfunding is still a new commercial form globally, it has gained the attention of regulators, although the legislation of crowdfunding is still in the exploratory stage, not every detail in the crowdfunding operation is regulated. Identifiably, crowdfunding industry needs to take up more legal responsibility, the regulation has the duty to provide a framework of industrial standard, to protect funders. According to our interviews with platform operators, the indeterminacy of legislation becomes the biggest risk, they felt worried about possible over-regulation, which would hinder the development of the industry, without understanding the key concept of crowdfunding, regulators may set inapposite rules and make it more difficult for small businesses or project to raise funds. Lack of legislation also causes intentional criminality. Some participants may conduct criminal activities under the guise of crowdfunding activities. As we introduced in the previous paragraph, the fraud is an inexcusable law breaking which has been already found in Crowding. Funders may not be warned timely, by the reason that some platforms do not become aware of the illegal behaviors effectively. Many platforms publish declarations, in order to avoid joint obligation, that they offer an intermediary service without carrying responsibility for default, failure in equity investment, guarantees for credit risk, or other liability for legal risks. However, platforms refuse to take responsibilities for investors' losses, extreme events still may turn into big reputational issues for platforms.

The legal risk also exists for initiators. Crowdfunding is very often used to finance innovative ideas. In order to let funders understand investment opportunities, initiators need to explain project details as much as possible. The probability of losing intellectual properties is enhanced.

## Chapter 4.2 - Characteristics of Risks in Crowdfunding

As one of Internet-based finance models, crowdfunding combines financial activities with the Internet technology. On one side, it inherits nearly all risk types of financial industry, on the other side, these risks show own characteristics and features.

- Systematic risks

In crowdfunding, funders invest corporately, the large number of investors and the small funding amount of each individual spread individual's risks and the risks in one single project. The credit risk is born associatively, the impact of unsystematic risk is reduced. Therefore, risks in crowdfunding are mainly systematic risks, the risk management in crowdfunding focuses much on the spreading systematic risks, which makes the diversification a good strategy.

- High requirement for regulation

Based on characteristics of crowdfunding that transactions, payments, services are executed online, financial activities through crowdfunding are not limited by time and location, transactions can be processed quickly, participants do not have to show physically, information asymmetric may exists for regulators. All these features enhance the difficulty of the supervision, especially the application of high technology requires regulation from more sections.

- High requirement for technology

Network security faces diverse threats such as hacker attacks, the diffusion of computer virus, data manipulations etc. Simultaneously crowdfunding involve in financial business, which may cause direct financial losses. Therefore, the security for crowdfunding is extremely important, the construction of firewalls and the technical risk management are highly demanded.

- High Diffusion

Crowdfunding has the ability to execute deals quickly, its intermediary service for financial activities are supported by powerful IT technology, it has also inherited the characteristic of Internet- high diffusion. As we analyzed in 4.1, crowdfunding faces entirely systematic risk, the high diffusion rate may cause the cross infection of risks and directly increases the costs of risk management.

## Chapter 4.3 - Risk Management in Crowdfunding

Although risks in crowdfunding are very diversified, any of them are hardly controlled by the individual funder. Platforms play important roles to provide protection for the crowdfunding participants, especially for funders.

Common policies to help funders reduce risks include setting limit for investment amounts over a period of time; setting the funding limit for companies, which can be raised through crowdfunding; due diligent and background check for projects, which seek funds via platforms; offering education in the risks specific knowledge to crowdfunding participants; holding reserve funds and preparing for extreme events such as default. The book introduces several management strategy and methods for specific risks in the following paragraphs.

### Chapter 4.3.1 - Market Risk Management

Crowdfunding platforms use two approaches to reduce market risk for customers. The most common method is reducing information asymmetry between initiators and funders, supporting participants with identification, measurement, selection and pricing risks. Prudential background checks and project selections by platforms can efficiently control risks. Platforms benefit from the big data technology and the cloud computing technology, and are able to build their analyses on the online collected data. If platforms have access to the high quality data source, information of credit ratings, archives of transaction records, platforms are able to save offline due diligence, which causes high transaction costs.

The second method to manage market risks is the diversification. Funders implement the idea of portfolio management, and invest in multiple selected initiators or projects to spread risks. We analyze the effect of the diversification with the Capital Asset Pricing Model (CAPM). We assume that, the platform has „n"projects to be invested in, the expected return of a project „i" is represented by „$R_i$", we invest equably in „n" projects, the portfolio return is calculated as followed:

$$R = \frac{1}{n}\sum_{i=1}^{n} Ri$$

According to CAPM, the expected return is calculated with the time value of the invested capital, is represented with risk free rate ($r_f$) and Beta $\beta$, which measure the risk in each project. We assume that, Beta $\beta$ represents the systematic risk for „n" projects, and the unsystematic risk rate is represented with $\varepsilon$. Enable to only focus on the unsystematic risk, we simplify the formula and take out the time value. The return of „i" can be calculated with:

$$R_i = \beta \cdot R_m + \varepsilon_i$$

We assume that, the market return $R_m$ is given, the systematic risk $\beta$ is constant and is not related to the individual project „$E[\varepsilon i \mid Rm] = 0$", the unsystematic risk $\varepsilon_i$ is randomly distributed under the conditions: mean= 0 and variance= $\sigma^2$. The expected return of the portfolio is calculated with:

$$R_p = \beta \cdot R_m + \frac{1}{n}\sum_{i=1}^{n} \varepsilon i$$

We assume that „n" is extremely big, the return of portfolio is almost distributes as: $\beta \cdot R_m + N(0, \frac{\sigma^2}{n})$. According to the law of large numbers, the return of portfolio has the convergence in probability:

$$\text{plim } R \mid R_m = \beta \cdot R_m$$

Through this formula above, we conclude that the bigger the diversification, the smaller the unsystematic market risk. It confirms, that the diversification is the most appropriate approach for crowdfunding platforms to reduce the influence of the market risk in individual projects.

### Chapter 4.3.2 - Credit Risk Management

The diversification is also an effective method to manage credit risk. Platforms set limits of the investment amount in one project, in order to force funders diversify their investments into more projects. The impact of this diversification is verified with the following mathematic model.

We assume that, there are „n" loans, the return rate of loan „i" is represented by „$L_i$". We invest equably in „n" loans, the return of the portfolio is:

$$L = \frac{1}{n}\sum_{i=1}^{n} L_i$$

We assume that all loans have the same interest rate „$\mu$", the same default probability „PD" and the given losses„ LGD". The loan „i" has the return:

$$L_i = \mu \text{ ( if 1- PD)}$$
$$L_i = \text{- LGD (if PD)}$$
$$L_i^* = \begin{cases} 1 \ (default) \\ 0 \ (not\ default) \end{cases}$$

Which leads to:

$$L_i = \mu - (\mu + LGD)\, L_i^*$$

The return of the whole portfolio is calculated with:

$$L = \mu - (\mu + LGD)\, L^*$$

Asymptotic Single Risk Factor (ASRF) Model can be used to measure portfolio credit risk[71], the correlation coefficient of different assets is given as „ $\rho$", the

[71] cf. Basel Committee on Banking Supervision

Basel Accord defines the $\rho$ as $0.12(2\text{-}\frac{1-e^{-50PD}}{1-e^{-50}})$

$$F(x) = Pr(L^* \leq x) = \phi(\frac{\sqrt{1-\rho}\,\phi^{-1}(x) - \phi^{-1}(PD)}{\sqrt{\rho}})$$

If the $x \approx -LGD$, the probability of losing is calculated as:

$$Pr(L < x) = Pr(L^* > \frac{\mu-x}{\mu+LGD}) = 1 - F(\frac{\mu-x}{\mu+LGD})$$

Mathematically, if $x \approx -LGD$, $\frac{\mu-x}{\mu+LGD} \approx 1$, which leads to the result:

$$Pr(L < x) = 1 - F(\frac{\mu-x}{\mu+LGD}) \approx 0$$

The formula above shows that, the probability of extreme events causing by credit risk is reduced to near zero, it confirms that the diversification is the appropriate approach to minimize the credit risk.

With the decreasing of the information asymmetry in crowdfunding, the risk identification, the measurement and the pricing become efficient, the transparency and the effectiveness of the market mechanism increase. Additionally, the diversification reduces the requirement for risk hedging, derivatives have been developed more simplified and standardized. The insurance model is still feasible for crowdfunding. There are some security companies, who offer the compensation insurance and gain from the insurance premium, some crowdfunding platforms offer the access to these security products as intermediaries. Another possibility of risk transfer is asset-backed third party guarantee. Initiators or lenders pledge their property to a third party, in order to obtain a security, this third party secures the repayment of obligations. The guarantee attracts more investors to join the crowdfunding, it minimizes risks of the individual. The risk transfer through third- party service is a popular way to manage risks in crowdfunding.

On the other hands, instead of having a third party such as insurance company, many crowdfunding platforms charge a small amount premium in proportion with the investment amount, they pool resources together, create a financial reserve and cover the loss of individual. The premium payment is adjusted and corresponded with the default probability. Taking the risk from funders is an efficient way to win investors' trust, but it may also easily accumulate the risk of platforms. Platforms need to estimate the default probability very carefully. This model allows platforms effectively manage credit risks for other actors.

### Chapter 4.3.3 - Operational Risk Management

By setting up an internal control system, the operational risk can be effectively managed. Prudent customer identification, background check, record analyses, data protection mechanism are important duties of platforms. The adequate internal management system of crowdfunding platforms enables to reduce the probability of loss from internal- and external fraud, behavior risk, legal risk etc.

The behavior management is an important approach to avoid operational risk. Platforms have to behavior neutrally, they are not supposed to financially involve in any projects and transactions, and they do not play roles either as initiators or as funders. Based on the crowdfunding theory, platforms are neutral intermediaries, they are responsible for the infrastructure of crowdfunding and may reduce risks for other participants. The education is another efficient method to improve the risk management performance. By posting lessons and specific knowledge through platforms, the risk sensitivity of funders and initiators may be enhanced and professional skill of the individual in risk management may be increased.

Crowdfunding is based on the data technology, intermediaries collect information, analyze customer behavior and pool a huge amount of data, the working process challenges their abilities in the network security and the data protection. Most platforms focus much on their security mechanism and the technological development, which acquire a big part of operational expenses, but it is the most direct way to manage the technological risk.

In order to prevent the fraud risk, some crowdfunding platforms demand the initiators to deposit a part of raised funds as financial reserve, this percentage of raised funds is used to carry the potential loss. In case that the fraud appears, platforms intervene actively and take necessary legal steps to recover the loss.

## Chapter 4.4 - Platform Solution and Cases

This book selects five cases and analyses them qualitatively. We intend to have an insight about the sense of the responsibility of crowdfunding platforms, existing risk management approaches, variations in resources and strategies, and determinants across different models.

During the research, we find out that the influence of cultural differences and the regulation discrepancy cannot be ignored, in order to take this factor in consideration, we choose crowdfunding platforms from four countries- US, UK, Germany, and China.

### Chapter 4.4.1 – FundersClub

Source: Fundersclub[72]

- Company profile

In the US, the crowdfunding industry especially the equity crowdfunding is regulated with the Jumpstart Our Business Start-ups (JOBS) Act and supervised by the Securities and Exchange Commission (SEC). FundersClub is one of typical equity crowdfunding platforms.

FundersClub is based in California, it defines itself as a „online venture capital fund", offers an online marketplace for accredited investors to benefit from a big range of start-ups, allows funders to build a diversified portfolio. On the

[72] Fundersclub<https://fundersclub.com/>, date of access: 02.12.2015

other hand, FundersClub gives entrepreneurs the access to financial resources and added value. FundersClub uses legal structures from angel groups and VC firms. Till today, it has acquired more than 12.000 accredited investors, invested more than $27 million in 108 companies, and it has a great performance with 47.9% net IRR[73]. Enable to invest through FundersClub, funders are required to go through the sign-up process and be verified that, they have a minimum income or net wealth. After the accreditation, they have the access to pre-screened start-ups, and are able to view all companies' profiles. Once funders decide to invest into a project, they can easily transfer the money by entering accounts' information, the platform secures the transaction process. Sometime an additional investors' verification is required to ensure the accreditation. After the transaction, funders are informed constantly about the development of projects.

FundersClub attracts a lot of professional investors from over 25 countries, includes angel investors, early employees of big companies, senior entrepreneurs, and famous venture capitalists.

- Risk management

FundersClub cares much about risk management for their funders, it has standardized a service line to help funders being acquainted with risks and reduce risks for them.

First of all, the platform requests an accreditation of investors to ensure the risk taking ability, which is required by JOBS. Only funders with at least $200.000 annual incoming or $1 million net worth are able to join the equity investment. In some cases, the platform even double-checks the accreditation. Additionally, FundersClub creates an education center to increase the risk awareness of funders.

Diversifying funder's portfolio is an important approach for investors to reduce unsystematic risks. Unlike other venture capital firms, this crowdfund-

[73] Fundersclub < https://fundersclub.com>, date of access: 30.01.2015

ing platform demands a much lower minimum check size. It enables their funders to easily build a diversified portfolio.

Compare to other crowdfunding platforms, FundersClub has a strict selection process for the start-ups, it does online and offline pre-screens, due diligences for every application. The project valuation focuses much on the market potential. Every application has to offer a large quantity of details such as market information, business model analyses, backgrounds of management team etc. Although the platform has higher threshold, it has won the funders' confident and increase the users' viscosity.

The Q&A forum of the platform ensures the communication between broader communities of start-ups and funders, it makes investors easily measure the business performance. Another service of the platform is networking events, funders and entrepreneurs may meet personally and expand the synergy.

### Chapter 4.4.2 – Indiegogo

Source: Indiegogo[74]

[74] Indigogo<https://www.indiegogo.com/>, date of access： 02.12.2015

- Company profile

In order to observe the risk management in different business models, we analyzed a reward-based crowdfunding Indiegogo. Indiegogo is a US based crowdfunding platform, founded in 2008. Now it becomes one of representatives for the crowdfunding industry.

Compare to its competitor, another reward-based crowdfunding Kickstarter, Indiegogo allows companies, governmental organizations, communities, or individuals to raise fund through them, the platform does not focus on any specific industry or a type of project. It also adopts a flexible funding model, that if the target amount is not reached, the initiator will still get the raised fund. Because of its flexibility, Indiegogo grows rapidly in the global market, but it has also got a high percentage of failed campaigns 80%[75]. Not yet has Indiegogo offered equity crowdfunding, and it does not allow any financial return for funders. Because of its business model, Indiegogo does not have to face the credit risk, the liquidity risk or even the market risk, but the operational risk still exists, the risk of fraud, the risk of projects' failure, the legal risk may affect the funders' confidence.

- Risk management

With low barriers for projects' entry, Indiegogo has been seen as less trustworthy than its competitor Kickstarter. Indiegogo develops several service lines to increase the funders' trust.

Indiegogo focuses much on the offline education, it organizes different courses for initiators and funders. Customer-relation managers and product managers educate their users face to face with the topics such as how to set goals, how to promote in Indiegogo, how to respond funders etc. Additionally, users can join different seminars. Another useful management tool is the knowledge management, Indiegogo has established a working group to sum up successful experiences to be shared with other participants. It attracts a big amount of

[75] Cf. Jeffries: <http://www.theverge.com/2013/8/7/4594824/less-than-10-percent-of-projects-on-indiegogo-get-fully-funded>, date of access: 31.01.2015

high-quality initiators to raise fund for their ideas.

The optional „Crowdfunding insurance" is tried out by Indiegogo, which allows funders to purchase an additional insurance to transfer risk of fail or risk of fraud. This insurance is directly provided by Indiegogo, project initiators are not involved in compensation. If funded projects fail, if promised rewards do not arrive in three months after funding, funders do not have to take the consequence, they get their investment repaid. This service is still in its test period and trailed with one project „Olive stress monitor wristband ". Once the crowdfunding insurance is implemented as a conventional product, it may increase the competitive strength of Indiegogo.

### Chapter 4.4.3 – Crowdcube

crowdcube

Source: Crowdcube[76]

- Company profile

In the UK, the equity crowdfunding and debt crowdfunding are categorized into the financial service industry, and they are regulated by the independent non-governmental organization Financial Conduct Authority (FCA). The regulation requires capital reserves against the extreme loss. FCA only allows sophisticated or qualified funders to join investment-based crowdfunding activities. On the other side, UK government also engages in incentives for the equity investment, Enterprise Investment Scheme (EIS) and Seed Enterprise Investment Scheme (SEIS) are both programs, which support the equity invest-

[76] Crowdcube<https://www.crowdcube.com/>, date of access: 02.12.2015

ment with perks and tax reliefs to reduce financial risks and balance the potential loss of investors.

Crowdcube is an authorized equity crowdfunding platform in UK. The platform is backed by the famous venture capital firm Balderton Capital, it has acquired 127.615 investors, successfully funded 188 businesses with nearly £ 55 million[77]. The minimum investment amount in Crowdcube is £10, which allows investors to diversify their portfolio and invest in more businesses. All applications have to be background checked and go through a due diligence process, once the application is proven, it has to specify the target amount and the percentage share in return for the raised fund. If the target amount is not reached within the time period, no money will be taken from funders. Once the pitch hits the target amount, investors will receive the adopted articles of association, they are still legally protected to withdraw their investments in the so-called „cooling off period ".

- Risk management

The same as FundersClub, Crowdcube only accepts investors with the risk taking ability, the platform only targets experienced investors. Funders have to satisfy the requirement of the industrial regulator and pass the test of risk awareness.

Enable to avoid legal risk, the platform only accepts investors from UK and a few other countries, where investors are legally entitled to invest in UK based businesses and are legally allowed to receive financial promotions.

Forcing funders to diversify their investment is also the prior approach for Crowdcube to minimize risks for their participants. Lower minimum investment amount, a large variety of businesses make funders more flexible. Beside the equity investment, FundersClub also provides investment opportunities in debts for cautious investors. The product „Mini-bonds "offers an attractive fixed-rate income and a quite secured repayment at the end of the term. It

---

[77] Crowdcube< https://www.crowdcube.com>, date of access: 30.01.2015

enormously avoids the market risk and the small business risk.

The professional fund management is a highlight product of Crowdcube. Accredited funders are able to join the venture funds and let professionals manage their portfolio. In order to minimize the probability of loss, Crowdcube carries out the pre-investment due diligence, the continuous monitoring of performance, the platform works closely with enterprises and reports the progress to investors every six months. A report of the portfolio performance is also provided continuously. The professional fund management efficiently reduces risks for individuals, who have less investment experiences or fewer sources.

The discussion Forum is used to enable the communication between funders and initiators, and between funders and funders. It helps investors to maximize resources and gain more information for their decision-makings. Another communication tool „Alternative Offer Tool" is developed by Crowdcube, which allows investors propose their business valuation and request for an adjustment for the initial offering. It enables investors to actively involve in business risk measurement and adjustment.

## Chapter 4.4.4 – Bettervest

Source: Bettervest[78]

- Company profile

As we introduced in the second chapter, the German Federal Government has polished the revised draft of the German Retail Investors' Protection Act (Kleinanlegerschutzgesetz) in November 2014, which increases the requirement for crowdfunding. The new draft sets limit for the maximum investment amount in one project and sets limit for the total investment amount of an investor. Although the draft is not yet adopted by the Federal Council, it has raised a dust inside the industry. But the draft only targets the equity based crowdfunding, because according to the German Investment Products Act (German: Vermögensanlagengesetz), the debt is not qualified as an investment product, brokers of debts are only required with a straightforward license under the German Trade, Commerce and Industry Regulation Act[79].

Bettervest is a German-based crowdfunding platform, it is the world's first debt-based crowdfunding platform for renewables and energy efficiency projects. Through the platform, lenders get access to relative secured investment opportunities, invest in energy- saving and cost-saving projects from non-governmental organizations, companies, communities etc. Lenders gain from the attractive fixed interest rate, which is much higher than a normal interest rate for deposits in banks, and they get repaid at the end of the term. All applications need to be analyzed by an independent energy efficiency consultant,

[78] Bettervest<https://www.bettervest.de/home>, date of access: 02.12.2015

[79] European Crowdfunding Networt 2013: 11

once the project has been approved, the application is listed in the platform until the target amount is reached, the project can be realized.

Bettervest focuses on the domestic market, because Germany has a potential of €53 billion in energy saving actives annually[80], the business has an attractive market capability, it is not worth to take more risks from the international expansion yet. Compare to other crowdfunding platforms, the platform gives funders an opportunity to support the environmental protection directly, which leads to a positive sense of pleasure.

- Risk management

Bettervest selects the low risk business intentionally, funders face much lower risks than if they invest in start-ups or personal loans. Funded projects are not responsible for the business success, but for the cost saving, which is quite predictable. Although the operational risk still exists, but the risk of fraud, the new business risk and the reputational risk are minimized through the business model of the platform.

Bettervest sets a line of conditions for organizations, which want to raise funds for their projects. Organizations must have a stable business performance, they have to be evaluated by the credit rating agency Bürgel or Schufa, only companies with the smallest default risk can get to the second step- projects evaluation. Bettervest only accepts projects, which are analyzed and calculated by the energy efficiency consultant. Projects have to show specific characteristic: small, simple, and low risky. Through the third party rating, Bettervest can easily measure the market risk, the credit risk and a part of the operational risk, and can reduce risks through the selection of projects for their funders.

The target amount is set to meet the financial need of realizing the energy efficiency project, it is accurately priced by the energy efficiency consultant and should be supported by the platform. Bettervest strictly controls the using of

[80] Bettervest <https://bettervest.de/de>, date of access: 30.01.2015

the raised fund, in order to be sure, that the capital is not used for other purposes and prevent the risk of fraud.

According to our personal interview with the CEO Patrick Mijnals, Bettervest has efficiently reduced types of risks, which their funders have to face. The biggest risk for investors is still the operational risk, Bettervest voluntarily involves in the projects' operation to actively control the operational risk. For the involvement, Bettervest charges an annual handing fee from project owners.

### Chapter 4.4.5 - Angelcrunch 天使汇

Source: Angelcrunch [81]

- Company profile

In January 2015, Securities Association of China (SAC) published the revise for the initial draft of the Equity Crowdfunding Regulation Act (私募股权众筹融资管理办法(试行)(征求意见稿)), the revised version reduces the requirement for the minimum investment amount in one project and reduces the requirement for the investors' accreditation. Although SAC has lowered the threshold for investment via crowdfunding, ordinary people still have difficulties to satisfy the requirement. The bright side of the China's draft is that, crowdfunding is categorized as an own industry and will be regulated separately.

From the market perspective, the lack of trusts hinders the enthusiasm of long tern investors to join crowdfunding, on the other side, the speculation becomes the main motivation for the participation, which makes initiators and funders hardly match each other. Despite all facts， there are approximately 122 crowdfunding platforms established in China till November 2014, 27 of them

[81] Angelcrunch<http://angelcrunch.com/>, date of access: 02.12.2015

are equity based.[82] This research chooses Angelcrunch for case studies, because it is the largest equity crowdfunding platform in China currently, and it has successfully funded many well-known enterprises.

Angelcrunch was founded in November 2011, as given by the name, professional angel investors are the target group of the platform. Angelcrunch has a team of business analysts and had adopted many working modes from angel investments. China's most famous angel investors have joined the platform, for example Jun Lei, the CEO of Xiaomi Inc., Hongwei Zhou, the founder of Qihoo 360. In three years, Angelcrunch has acquired 2177 accredited investors, funded ¥3 billion in 302 projects. Its tagline is „we connect best start-ups with smart money", which explains two features of the platform: 1) compare to other platforms, Angelcrunch cares much about qualifications of funders and their previous experiences, that's the reason that, Angelcrunch obtains the attention of industrial insiders rapidly. 2) Angelcrunch focuses much on the added value for entrepreneurs, and provides numerous supporting services. After receiving applications, the analysts team does the rounded due diligence, it helps entrepreneurs with Business-plans, coordinates projects to suitable funders, arranges meetings between initiators and funders etc. Angelcrunch funded many successful projects such as Didi Dache, which is a taxi-hailing App raised ¥15 million in Angelcrunch, and it has raised $ 700 million from global investors in the recent round[83].

- Risk management

Like other platforms, Angelcrunch focus much on the risk taking ability of funders and only allows „smart money"to be invested. The platform defines the „smart money"as the surplus capital from investors, who have to have the ability of risk identification and management. Therefor the accredited funders in Angelcrunch are normally sophisticated angel investors. Nearly all funded projects in Angelcrunch have a leading investor, who has professional backgrounds in the specific industry, and supports entrepreneurs with their long-term experiences. The joint investment efficiently reduces risks for individual

[82] cf.iiMedia Research Group <http://www.iimedia.cn/38502.html>, date of access: 31.01.2015, translated by the author

[83] Angelcrunch <http://angelcrunch.com>, date of access: 31.01.2015, translated by the author

investors, who have less specific knowledge for the invested industry.

Angelcrunch also lays emphasis on the diversification. It repeats the importance of the risk diversification many times in its platform, although funders are mainly professional angel investors.

For the selection of applications, Angelcrunch has a strict requirement for the information disclosure, all projects have to publish details as the platform demands, the feasibility of each business is analyzed by the professional team. A double check from investors is also expected from the platform. All entrepreneurs have to meet their potential investors personally, meetings are coordinated by the platform to deepen the examination and the valuation from the funders' perspective, enable funders to identify potential risks and choose right projects.

Angelcrunch has designed a so-called „start-ups swap ", the simple explanation is that, if one project fails, entrepreneurs may still be paid with six months' salaries to encourage them to try the next business venture. As terms of exchange, the investment amount in the failed project is converted as shares in the second project with a swap ratio of 1:0.7. It helps funders to reduce losses of the new business risk.

### Chapter 4.4.6 - Case Study Conclusion

This research analyses five chosen cases, focuses on their business models and existing risk management approaches. These platforms implement diverse risk management strategies, based on different cultural backgrounds, regulations, characteristics of business and funders.

All five platforms are well preformed, have a stable business development, and have standardized services. All equity-based or debt-based platforms only accept domestic applicants, in order to ensure the background 's check and the risk measurement. The limitation for the investment amount in the single project is quite different, as well as the requirement of the minimum investment amount in one project.

We summarize all risk management approaches of each platform into one matrix, in order to analyze statistically. Based on our case analyses[84], we find out that the diversification is the most used approach and the most effective method to reduce risks in crowdfunding, all equity-based and debt-based crowdfunding platforms implement this approach to diversify risks for funders, they create necessary conditions for funders. The strict projects' selection is another chosen way to control risk, all equity- and debt-based platforms do background checks and business valuations, rejecting risky projects is an effective way to avoid risks for funders. Crowdfunding operators do not only select applications, 60% of our cases even choose investors and only accept accredited funders. Additional services also help platforms to reduce potential risks for other participants and increase their service quality. Every platform offers different services based on their investors' characteristics. Building connections between initiators and funders is the most offered service. Risk sharing is not often used in the chosen cases, none of equity- or debt based crowdfunding platforms uses the risk transfer approach.

[84] Exhibit 4. Summary of risk management approaches of case studies

Exhibit 4. Summary of risk management approaches in case studie

| RM Approaches \ Platforms | | Funders-Club | Indie-gogo | Crowd cube | Better-vest | Angel-crunch | Sum |
|---|---|---|---|---|---|---|---|
| | | Equity based | Re-wards - based | Equity based | Debt based | Equity based | |
| Diversi-fication | Small minimum invest-ment amount, large va-riety of business | X | | X | X | X | 4 |
| | Diversified product-portfolio management | | | X | | | 1 |
| Risk transfer | Insurance | | X | | | | 1 |
| Risk Avoid-ance | Low risk business model | | | | X | | 1 |
| | Application selection, reject risky business | X | | | X | X | 3 |
| | Reject overseas funders or initiators | | | X | X | | 2 |
| | Accreditation of inves-tors | X | | X | | X | 3 |
| | Third party valuation | | | | X | | 1 |
| Addi-tional services | Communication chan-nel between funders and initiators | X | | X | | X | 3 |
| | Offering education | | X | | | | 1 |
| | Involvement in projects' operation | | | | X | X | 2 |
| | Start-ups Swaps | | | | | X | 1 |

# Chapter 5 - Conclusion

The development of crowdfunding has its history inevitability. The widespread using of computers and Internet builds the crowdfunding a good foundation to make great progresses. Through crowdfunding, entrepreneurs can easily present their projects, and rapidly reach potential funders. Simultaneously, funders have the access to a wide range of investment opportunities, and can diversify their portfolio with lower transaction costs. With access to the database and the information pool, which provided by crowdfunding operators, funders are able to select projects themselves. Crowdfunding becomes a new model to fund businesses, ideas and projects. Based on its characteristics such as the automated information collecting and the analyzing through big data technology, many economists forecast that, the crowdfunding will lead the next revolution in the financial industry. But potential threats to the stability of financial market, which may be caused by the crowdfunding, cannot be ignored.

As an alternative fund raising model, crowdfunding brings huge opportunities to the macro-economic, it may solve financing problems of SMEs and may inspire entrepreneurships. But it also challenges the regulation. According to this research, to remain the healthy development of the crowdfunding industry, the rapid modification of regulatory policies and deep engagement of a wide range of stakeholders are requested[85]. It is essential for regulators to create an infrastructure for the crowdfunding industry.

As a rising star in the financial industry, crowdfunding has necessity to be focused as an individual academic ambit. We assume that, an independent research institute with veracious data and information, which provided by crowdfunding operators, will provide the industry valuable references to establish a standard, and will drive the industry growth.

The education also plays an important role, the industry will benefit from the continue enhancing of knowledge level of platform operators, entrepreneurs (initiators) and investors (funders). Entrepreneurs will be able to improve their

[85] cf. European Crowdfunding Framework: 5

projects and businesses, funders may manage their investments in the better way, crowdfunding intermediaries are able to increase the service quality, to satisfy the market demand, to provide integrated products, and to enhance own economic value.

Although the crowdfunding industry still has a small size of market scale, but it has already threatened the market position of the traditional financial industry, and has gained the public attention. The high degree of acceptance and the high degree of percolation may continuously advance the development of crowdfunding. Healthy competition drives the development, which can never be paid with the sacrifice of customers. Reducing risks and protecting users become the most important duty of crowdfunding operators, their attitude and the ability of risk management directly affects the industry' reputation and the popularity.

According to this case study, there is no standardization of risk management strategies in crowdfunding, each platform assesses own business models, defines the goal of risk management, measures involved risks, valuates different methods and chooses most suitable approaches. The risk diversification, the third-party rating, the strict selection and the timely rejection, the optional insurance etc. are risk management approaches, which are favored by crowdfunding intermediaries and used to minimize risks for other participants.

This book focuses on the most significant theme in finance „risk management", and combines the risk management with the new form of financing „crowdfunding". It is the first time in the industry to target the question „how could intermediaries reduce risks for crowdfunding participants?" from a rather macroscopic perspective. In order to analyze deeply, I combine different research methods such as case study, personal interviews, and theory construction study. Still the research is far away from consummation, the crowdfunding as a new phenomenon needs to be observed constantly. This research looks forward to trigger more interests of academia.

# Bibliography


United States Government Accountability Office. Person-to-Person Lending, New Regulatory Challenges Could Emerge as the Industry Grows[R] .2011.

Crowdfunding Industry Report: Market Trends, Composition and Crowdfunding Platforms. Crowdsourcing.org. May,2012

Benedikt, M (2013): Rechtliche Aspekte von Crowdfunding. Wien, Wirtschaftsuniv., Dipl.-Arb.

Czafik, R (2014): Activities and roles of crowdinvestors in overcoming the liabilities of newness and smallness of start-ups. Wien, Wirtschaftsuniv., Master-Arb.

Forster, M (2013): Crowdfinancing - (k)eine Finanzierungsalternative für Start-ups und Jungunternehmen? Trauner

Gremel, A (2013): Informationsasymmetrien bei der Finanzierung durch Crowdfunding. Wien, Wirtschaftsuniv., Dipl.-Arb.

Hemer, J (2011): Crowdfunding und andere Formen informeller Mikrofinanzierung in der Projekt- und Innovationsfinanzierung. Stuttgart： Fraunhofer-Verlage

Tenambergen, A（2012）： Erfolgsfaktoren von Web-basiertem Crowdfunding. Wien, Wirtschaftsuniv., Dipl.-Arb.

Winkler, A (2014): Relationships & trust between actors in crowd investing. Wien, Wirtschaftsuniv., Master-Arb.

Lars, S; Björn B; Fili, A (2013) : Increasing the Heterogeneity and Competition of Early Stage Financing: An Analysis of the Role of Crowdfunding in Entrepreneurial Ventures. World Academy of Science, Engineering and Technology International Journal of Social, Management, Economics and Business Engineering

2013 CF: The Crowdfunding Industry Report. Massolution and Crowdsourcing.org

Liu,Y; Luo, M (2014): Internet based financing models and risks related regulation. Beijing: China Academic Journal

Hu, J; Wu Y( 2013): Development of crowdfunding and its regulation. Beijing University, Huanghua Business School.

De Buysere, K; Gajda, O; Kleverlaan,R; Marom, D (2012): A Framework for European Crowdfunding. www.crowdfundingframework.eu

De Manuel, M (2014): Investor Protection and Crowdfunding. CFA Institute Magazine

Zheng, J; Wan, N; Chen, D; Wang, T: Antecedents of project implementation success in crowdfunding, working paper

Ramos, J (2014): Crowdfunding and the Role of Managers in Ensuring the Sustainability of Crowdfunding Platforms. JRC Scientific and Policy reports.

Sannajust, A; Roux, F; Chaibi, A (2014): Crowdfunding In France: A New Revolution? Working Paper 2014-234. Ipag Business School

Crowdsourcing.org (2012): Crowdfunding industry report: Market Trends, Composition and Crowdfunding Platforms.

Collins, L (2014): Crowdfunding: Innovative access to finance and regulatory challenges. World bank

Meeuwsen,R (2013): Crowd Funding & Renewable Energy Projects. Delft University of Technology, Masterwork.

Connor, S: Crowdfunding's Impact on Start-up in Strategy. University of Washington School of Law

Schacht, K (2014): Does Crowdfunding Pose a Threat to Investors? CFA Institute Magazine

Hui, J; Gerber, E; Greenberg, M (2012): Easy Money? The Demands of Crowdfunding Work. Northwestern University, Segal Design Institute, Technical Report No. 4

Pazowski, P; Czudec, W (2014): Economic Prospects and Conditions of Crowdfunding. Management, Knowledge and learning International Conference 2014: Human Capital without Borders. Working Paper

Ley, A; Weaven, S (2011): Exploring Agency Dynamics of Crowdfunding in Start-up Capital financing. Academy of Entrepreneurship Journal, Volume 17, Number 1

Stiernblad,M; Skoglund, E (2013): The Future of Equity Crowdfunding– Is "The Crowd" Capable of Good Investment? Lund University, Degree Project Master of Science in Business and Economics

Agrawal, A; Catalini, C; Goldfarb, A (2011): The Geography of Crowdfunding. Cambridge: National Bureau of Economic Research, Working Paper 16820

Ahlers, G; Cumming, D; Günther, C; Schweizer, D: Signaling in Equity Crowdfunding. Working papers

Mollick, E (2014): The dynamics of crowdfunding: An exploratory study Journal of Business Venturing 29 (2014) 1–16

Pesok, J: Crowdfunding: A new Form of Investing requires a new Form of Investor . University of Minnesota Law School. Working papers

Rossi, M (2014): The New Ways to Raise Capital: An Exploratory Study of Crowdfunding. International Journal of Financial Research, Vol. 5, No. 2; 2014

Guo, Q : The practical use of Crowd funding, Two cases illustration. Lund University, School of Economics and Management. Master thesis

Zhang, J (2013): The Wisdom of Crowdfunding. MIT Sloan school of management.

Smith, L: Crowdfunding and using net worth to determine investment limits. Denver University Law

Li, T (2013): Fraud in Crowdfunding and Antifraud Insurance. The George Washington University Law School, working paper

Brydon, J; Ferguson, T; Hoang, J; Israel, A; Tulusan K (2012): Private-Equity Crowdfunding. SUS6175: Capital Markets, SP12

Moenninghoff, S; Wieandt, A(2012): The Future of Peer-to-Peer Finance. Zeitschrift für Betriebswirtschaftliche Forschung, August/September 2013, p. 466-487

Jorion, P; GARP (2007): Financial Risk Manager Handbook, 4th Edition. New Jersey: John Wiley & Sons

The State of Queensland: A Guide to Risk Management. July 2011

Hull, C (2012): Risk Management and Financial Institutions, Third Edition. New Jersey: Wiley

Manbeck, P; Hu, S(2014): The Regulation of Peer- to –Peer Lending: A summary of the Principal Issues (2014 Update)".

Ordanini, A; Miceli, L; Pizzeti, M; Parasuraman, A: Crowdfunding: Transforming Customers into Investors through innovative Service platforms. The Bocconi University: research paper.

Freedman, D; Nutting, M (2015): A Brief History of Crowdfunding: Including Rewards, Donation, Debt, and Equity Platforms in the USA. Educational Websites

Belleflamme, P; Lamber, T; Schwienbacher, A (2010): Crowdfunding: An Industrial Organization Perspective. Working paper for the workshop: Digital Business Models: Understanding Strategies

Zhang, Y (2012): An Empirical Study into the Field of Crowdfunding. Lund University, School of Economics and Management, Master Thesis in Accounting and Auditing

The World Bank (2013): Crowdfunding's Potential for the Developing World. Conference Version

Gerber, E; Hui, J; Kuo, P: Crowdfunding: Why People Are Motivated to Post and Fund Projects on Crowdfunding Platforms. Northwestern University, Creative Action Lab, working paper

Ma, C; Li, H; Xu, S; Yang, X; Li, H (2001): Total-parametric Methods of VaR and Its Application in Risk Management of Financial Market. Journal of Financial Engineering, Theory & Practice, April 2001, Article 1000-6788 (2001) 04-0074-06

Agrawal, A; Catalini, C; Goldfarb, A; Koven, M (2014): Comment on Key Provisions of the Proposed Crowdfunding Prospectus Exemption. Comment

Silver, L; Berggren, B; Fili, A (2013): Increasing the Heterogeneity and Competition of Early Stage Financing: An Analysis of the Role of Crowdfunding in Entrepreneurial Ventures. World Academy of Science, Engineering and Technology International Journal of Social, Management, Economics and Business Engineering Vol:7 No:1

Mollick, E (2014): The dynamics of crowdfunding: An exploratory study. Journal of Business Venturing: 29 (2014) 1–16

Liu, L (2013): Risks of P2P Lending and Regulation Issue in China. Journal of Credit Reference: No.11, 2013, Serial No. 178

Basel Committee on Banking Supervision (2005): International Convergence of Capital Measurement and Capital Standards. A Revised Framework

Basel Committee on Banking Supervision (2005): Enclosure 2: Specific comments related to Operational Risk

Keiding, H (2011): Basic Concept of Risk Management. Economics of Banking (Prel.version:August 11), Chapter 3

Ernst & Young (2008): Measuring operational risk.

Bervas, A: Market Liquidity and Its Incorporation into Risk Management. Banque de France, Financial Stability Review, No. 8

Hong Kong Monetary Authority: Supervisory Policy Manual: Strategic Risk Management. SR-1 V.1-12.12.07

Deloitte (2013): Exploring Strategic Risk: 300 executives around the world say their view of strategic risk is changing

Berger, S; Gleisner, F (2008): Emergence of Financial Intermediaries on Electronic Markets: The Case of Online P2P Lending. University of Frankfurt, working Paper

Ginsburg, M; Kambil, A (1999): A Web-based knowledge management support system for document collections, in Proceedings of HICSS-32

Dahlman, C (1979): The Problem of Externality. Journal of Law and Economics. Vol. 22 No.1, Apr., 1979

Röthler, D; Wenzlaff, K (2011): Crowdfunding Schemes in Europe. European Expert Network on Culture, EENC Report